GLOSTER
JAVELIN

Previous page: WD804 demonstrates its performance at height.

Below: Gloster Javelin F(AW) Mk 4, XA630 over the Cathedral City of Gloucester.

POSTWAR MILITARY AIRCRAFT:1

GLOSTER JAVELIN

MAURICE ALLWARD

LONDON

IAN ALLAN LTD

First published 1983

ISBN 0 7110 1323 3

Published by Ian Allan Ltd, Shepperton, Surrey;
and printed by Ian Allan Printing Ltd at their works
at Coombelands in Runnymede, England

Contents

Front cover: Javelin of No 23 Squadron, Coltishall, June 1960, ready for an in-flight refuelling practice sortie.

Back cover, top: Javelin F(AW) Mk 9 of No 23 Squadron on an accompanied flight to Karachi with a Valiant of No 214 Squadron during Exercise 'Pounce', June 1961.

Back cover, bottom: Javelin F(AW) Mk 9R of No 60 Squadron at Clark Field, Manila, Philippines, en route to Kai Tak, Hong Kong, June 1967.

Left: One of the production batch of 30 Javelin F(AW) Mk 2s. This particular aircraft, XA778, was fitted with Sapphire 7 engines as part of the Javelin 7 development programme. Later it was used for Pressure Error Correction work at Boscombe Down.

1

Javelin Genesis

The Javelin was conceived during that short period after World War 2 when Britain, spurred on by the political situation in Europe and the memory of Hiroshima in the Far East, achieved a measure of supremacy in fighter technology. The development of the high-flying jet bomber, coupled with the awesome power of the atomic bomb, posed an obvious threat to Britain that required precautions even though the blood of war was not yet dry.

Gloster Aircraft Company, having produced Britain's first jet-powered aircraft, the E28/39, and the Meteor, the only Allied jet aircraft to be used operationally during the war, was obviously keen to exploit the company's experience and reputation to increase its participation in the provision of the 'precautions'.

The E28/39 specification, issued in February 1940, stated: 'The primary object of this aeroplane will be to flight test the engine installation, but the design will be based on the requirements for a fixed-gun interceptor fighter as far as the limitations of size and weight imposed by the power unit permit. The armament equipment called for in this specification will not be required for the initial trials, but the contractor will be required to make provision in the design for the weight and space occupied by these items'.

The E28/39 flew for the first time on 15 May 1941 and the pioneering experience gained with this experimental aircraft complemented the operational flying obtained with the single-seat, twin-jet Meteor which

entered squadron service with the RAF in July 1944, and achieved its first 'kill' on 4 August when one knocked down a V-1 flying bomb with a wing tip. Success continued into peace, with the Meteor raising the world's speed record, first to 606mph in November 1945 and then to 616mph in September 1946. The Company had a two-and-half year lead over the up-coming de Havilland Vampire and was more than five years ahead of the Supermarine Attacker.

Some people pin-point the Javelin starting point with the issue of two Air Ministry specifications in January 1947, but others claim that the aircraft lineage can be traced back to earlier Gloster proposals made to the Ministry of Supply for developments of the Meteor.

The two 'datum' specifications were F43/46, which called for a highly manoeuvrable single-seat fighter, for the daylight interception and destruction of high-speed, high altitude bombers, and F44/46, for a two-seat night fighter, capable of intercepting enemy aircraft at heights up to at least 40,000ft.

It was the F44/46 specification from which the Javelin was conceived and so the official detail requirements are noteworthy. These included a maximum speed of not less than 525kts at 40,000ft, for the interception of enemy bombers flying at 480kts, with a service ceiling of 45,000ft.

A high rate of climb was required, this allowing less than 10 minutes from the time the pilot pressed the starter switch to the aircraft reaching 45,000ft. To

Left: A fine in-flight view of the prototype Javelin, WD804, showing to full advantage its classic delta wing and tailplane of similar planform.

Top: WD804 during an early flight. Of interest is the 'port-hole' visibility provided for the observer in the rear cockpit, and the anti-spin parachute fairing on the tailplane. The adjacent 'fences' were installed to prevent the shrouds jamming the elevators.

Above: An early 'secret' photograph of the prototype Javelin WD804, showing its nose-mounted pitot boom.

Left: W. A. Bill Waterton, Gloster chief test pilot, who did much of the early Javelin development flying.

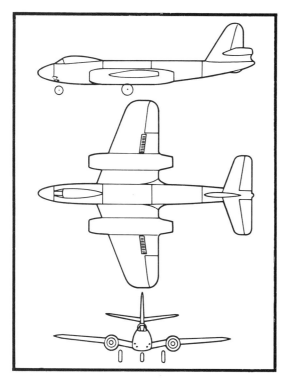

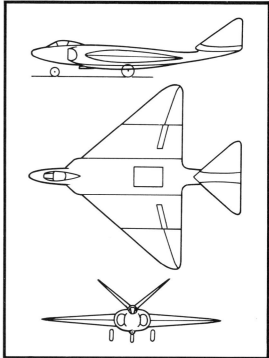

achieve this, very rapid starting was of prime importance, with an ideal start-up time of only five seconds between the pilot receiving the order to 'scramble' and the engines running at idle ready to be opened up for take-off.

The minimum endurance was two hours from take-off to landing, including taxying, climb to 25,000ft, 15min combat at that altitude, with the remainder of the time spent cruising at the same height.

Airbrakes were to operate in four seconds, take off was to be within a distance of 1,500yd, and landing in 1,200yd over a 50ft obstacle. Strength requirements called for 4g manoeuvres at top speed at sea level, and the pressure cabin was to be able to reproduce the pressure equivalent to 25,000ft at 45,000ft actual height.

Comprehensive equipment was specified, including multi-channel VHF radio, airborne interception radar, navigational aids and, possibly, blind landing equipment. Aids to crew comfort and safety included oxygen for 2.5hr at 25,000ft, a jettisonable cockpit canopy, ejection seats, dinghies and parachutes. Armament was to comprise four forward-firing 30mm guns, with sufficient ammunition for 15sec firing per gun.

Finally, it was required that the aircraft was to be suitable for economic production of 150 at a maximum rate of 10 units a month, and to be simple to

Above left: Gloster proposal P228, of 1946, for a two-seat night fighter to Spec F44/46. It was powered by two Rolls-Royce AJ65 engines and armed with four 30mm cannon. Its Meteor parentage is evident.

Above: Gloster proposal P234, dated February 1947, for a single-seat interceptor. One of the earliest proposals featuring a delta-wing, it was powered by two Rolls-Royce AJ65 engines and was armed with a single 40mm gun.

service to ensure a rapid turn-round time. The specification indicates the rapid advances made in fighter evolution since the 350kt Meteor 1s went into service only three years earlier.

During 1947 Glosters prepared a number of projects to meet these two specifications. Some of these, such as the P228 and P240 were of obvious Meteor parentage. However, Mr W. G. Carter, Gloster Chief Designer was, in common with other British designers, attracted by the potential of the delta wing layout, as a result of information received on German wartime work on this planform, particularly that of Dr Alexander Lippisch. Thus, some proposals, such as the P234, embodied this wing configuration; this particular project also embodying an unusual delta-Vee tailplane.

At this early postwar stage, the precise requirements of the RAF were subject to change, particularly

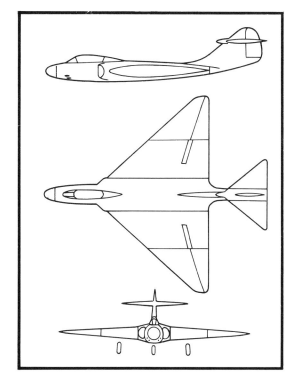

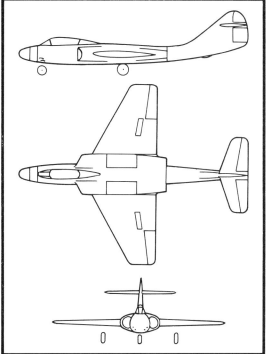

regarding armament and radar equipment, and in February 1948, the two specifications were superseded by specification F3/48 for a day fighter, and F4/48, for a night fighter. The Ministry originally hoped that a single basic design could be evolved suitable for both roles, but Gloster prepared two quite distinct types, the P272 and P275. The two-seat, twin-engined P272, designed to meet Specification F4/48, had a delta wing and a delta tailplane and was much bigger and heavier than the single-seat, single-engined P275, meeting Specification F3/48. In the P275 the pilot was unconventionally located in the leading edge of the sharply swept fin of a classic delta configuration without a tailplane. Both aircraft embodied rotating wing-tip controls, instead of ailerons, because of the sparse information then available on lateral control associated with delta wings. A brochure issued in April 1948, gives the all-up weight of the P272, powered by two Rolls-Royce Avon engines, as 25,500lb and the P275 as 18,500lb.

Later projects had conventional ailerons. Also, following information from the USA that conventional elevators were satisfactory on the North American Sabre at transonic speeds, the slab tailplanes of early projects were replaced by a fixed tailplane with elevators.

The changes in the Ministry Specification were accompanied by personnel changes at Glosters. In

Above left: Gloster proposal P238, dated March 1947, for a day and night interceptor. It was powered by two Metropolitan Vickers F9 engines. Armament was four 30mm cannon. Noteworthy features are the Meteor-like fuselage and the slab tailplane.

Above: Gloster proposal P240, prepared in April 1947 for a day and night interceptor, featured a 'plank'-wing with moderate sweepback.

January Mr Carter became technical director of the company, and direct responsibility for design work passed to his successor as chief designer, Mr Richard W. Walker. He was supported by Mr I. James, chief technician; Mr D. I. Husk, chief aerodynamicist and Mr J. F. Cuss, chief stressman. All these people were intimately concerned with the development of the design, under the overall direction of Mr P. G. Crabbe, the managing director.

With these changes, the decision was taken to concentrate on meeting specification F4/48 for the all-weather fighter. Further projects were schemed, including aircraft with two, three and four engines, and one with a single Rolls-Royce Avon engine and two 3,000lb thrust rocket motors. Throughout, these projects all employed a delta wing.

During the early development stage wind tunnel tests continued to refine the aerodynamic envelope of

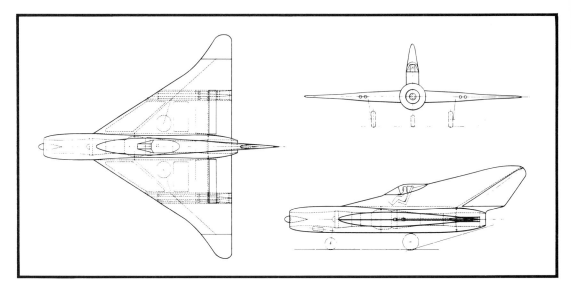

the aircraft. A wing thickness/chord ratio of 8% was extensively tested, but rejected because of the weight penalty involved. Finally, a ratio of 10% was chosen. At first the position of the maximum thickness of the wing was at 36% chord from the leading edge. However, tests with various maximum thickness positions on the same planform suggested it would be advantageous to move the maximum thickness further forward.

Other changes made as a result of wind-tunnel tests at high altitudes, included a modification to the fuselage lines in the region of the air intakes. Other tests resulted in a reduction in the taper of the tailplane planform, obtained by sweeping back the trailing edge which was originally at right angles to the fuselage centre-line.

In spite of the German data becoming available, little was known in Britain about the characteristics of swept wings at high speeds or the lift developed by the delta planform at low speeds. Particularly worrying were the misgivings about the stall characteristics, and those at high angles of attack at low speeds, particularly during landing.

The Ministry initiated, through the RAE, a full scale investigation into the delta wing, which eventually led to the construction of the Boulton Paul P111 research data. However, this did not fly until October 1950, so that the experience gained with this aircraft was too late to help the Gloster design team.

A. V. Roe was also busy creating a veritable fleet of delta wing research aircraft to provide basic data on the planform, but these were also too late to benefit Gloster, again serving merely to corroborate its established design features. The second Avro aircraft, the 707B, which made its first flight on 6 September 1950, did however give the Gloster chief test pilot the opportunity to fly a delta-wing aircraft and to experience some of the low-speed characteristics before undertaking the flight test programme on the F4/48.

In view of the unknowns regarding the handling characteristics, one might wonder at the attractions of the delta wing. It had several basic advantages over the conventional sweptback wing as embodied on one design study for the Javelin. The high taper ratio of the delta gave the low aspect ratio needed for a fighter, the sharp sweepback was good for high speeds, and the relatively generous wing area helped to meet the stringent take-off and high altitude performance requirements.

The long root chord gave a relatively thin wing combined with a large internal volume in which to accommodate the fuel, armament and retracted landing gear. The wing blended smoothly into the fuselage which was estimated to contribute about one fifth of the total wing lift.

From the structural point of view the delta was almost ideal, the high taper, low aspect ratio and depth of the wing root combining to give a low structure weight combined with maximum wing stiffness in bending and torsion.

For these reasons, the design was confirmed around the delta wing planform. A delta tailplane was mounted on top of a large swept fin, to cope with the trim changes anticipated through the wide speed range

of the aircraft. Provision of a tailplane also enabled use to be made of flaps, and eliminated the high-angle of attack touchdown usually associated with delta-wing aircraft — a great advantage for night operations.

The choice of powerplant was between a pair of Rolls-Royce AJ65 Avons, then developing 6,500lb thrust, or two Metrovick F.9s each of 7,000lb thrust. Later Armstrong Whitworth took over development of the Metrovick engine which became known as the Sapphire.

By July 1948 the design had stabilised around two 9,000lb thrust Sapphire 2 engines, but a further proposal increased the loaded weight to 29,200lb and the wing area from 900sq ft to 1,100sq ft. A month later, yet another proposal, Project P280, was made, reverting to a 900sq ft wing, and two 7,500lb thrust Sapphires. This engine was selected in preference to its Rolls-Royce competitor solely because of its greater thrust. It was a happy decision because the engine proved to be easy to install and gave very little trouble in service.

Concurrent with the Gloster work, de Havilland were also preparing a proposal the DH110, to the F4/48 Specification, and on 13 April 1949, the Ministry of Supply, issued instructions to both manufacturers to proceed with the construction of four prototypes, plus one airframe for structural testing.

The small number of prototypes was in accordance with established British practice, even though it was already evident that many more were necessary for an efficient development programme and to take care of any possible losses. However, even this pitiful quantity was reduced to two in November 1949, by the Labour Government then in power as an 'economy' measure. This was a classic example of political ineptitude

regarding aviation matters, for it was impossible to do all the development flying of such a complex aircraft on only two prototypes. In the event the reduction almost proved disastrous for the whole Javelin project, and at the very least delayed the entry of the aircraft into service by many months. That the reduction was a mistake, was in fact recognised within months, and on 22 March 1951 the order was increased to five F4/48 prototypes and one prototype of a trainer version.

However, the short-sighted vacillation of the Ministry completely disrupted the orderly process of design, manufacture and flight testing. Extra work was created in the Design Office, and work underway in the factory was dislocated. The reinstatement order came too late to prevent a break in development continuity and, as a result, the first production aircraft

11

was actually manufactured before the prototype order was complete.

Construction of the first prototype began immediately at the Company's experimental department of the wartime dispersal site at Bentham after receipt of the first MoS order in April 1949.

By February 1950 structural design work had been largely completed, and the systems drawings were issued by June 1950. A year later the first prototype was structurally complete, with an all-metal nose in place of the radome. The aircraft closely resembled the P280 in almost every aspect, the most noticeable difference being the absence of the large 'acorn' fairing at the intersection of the fin and tailplane. Wind tunnel testing had indicated that this was not necessary, and it was also omitted from all subsequent aircraft.

A noteworthy feature of the prototype was that the rear of the canopy enclosing the two tandem cockpits was 'solid', with only two small side 'portholes'. The observer was thus in semi-darkness, an environment also 'enjoyed' by the observer on the de Havilland DH110. Official thinking was that such conditions would enable the observer to concentrate on his radar equipment more efficiently.

The company designation by which the aircraft was usually known was GA5 and this should not be confused with other numbers prefixed by G which are sometimes allocated to the aircraft. The simple system of G numbers has been claimed to be the official method used by Glosters to designate aircraft types and sub-types, but this is not true. The 'G-system' was a reference system evolved by the company's publicity department in 1948, which discovered that if the prototype Gladiator, with the civil registration G37, was considered the 37th Gloster aircraft, then by working backwards, and applying numbers and suffix letters indiscriminately, it was possible to arrive at G1 for the Mars I, the company's first product!

In July the prototype fighter, serial number WD804, was moved from Bentham to the airfield at Moreton Valence. Then followed two months of reassembly, final equipping and preparation for flight work. This included the installation of the usual flight test instrumentation, and an anti-spin parachute housed in a streamlined fairing on top of the tailplane.

Flight testing was placed in the hands of Gloster's chief test pilot, Sqn Ldr W. 'Bill' A. Waterton AFC. This was preceded by a month of ground testing and taxying trials, during which about 30 high speed runs were made, resulting in the early embodiment of several modifications.

Finally on 26 November 1951, aircraft and weather were both satisfactory and, preceded by a Meteor chase aeroplane, WD804 took off for the first time.

12

Gloster F4/48 Night Fighter Weight Estimate (lb)

Power Unit	
Engines, 2 Avon c/w auxiliaries	4,400
Ducts	250
Jet pipes (c/w allowance for after-burning)	380
Engine mountings	40
Engine controls	10
Fuel tanks (800gal)	320
Fuel system	100
Power Unit	5,500

Fuel & Oil	
Fuel (630gal)	5,100
Oil (2½gal)	20
Fuel & Oil	5,120

Military Load	
4-4½in gun tubes and mountings	2,100
4 rounds ammunition	200
Pressurising and heating	100
Instruments and vacuum system	140
Oxygen system complete	80
TR1501	80
R3121	50
Rebecca	70
Blind landing equipment	70
AI	750
Gunsight with radar presentation	130
Electrical equipment	550
Pilot, parachute, dinghy and water cushion	220
Oberver, parachute, dinghy and water cushion	220
2 ejection seats	180
Engine fire protection	300
Fire extinguishers and systems	100
Inert gas system	120
G45 camera and mounting	10
Brake system	50
Auxiliary gearbox and mounting	60
Desert equipment	90
Miscellaneous	40
Military Load	5,710

Structure	
Wings	4,180
Tailplane	330
Fin and rudder	360
Fuselage	2,600
Undercarriage	1,020
Nosewheel	260
Flying controls	220
Hydraulics	200
Structure	9,170

All up weight	25,500

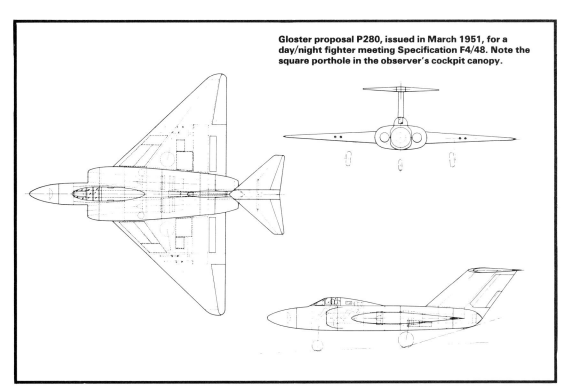

Gloster proposal P280, issued in March 1951, for a
day/night fighter meeting Specification F4/48. Note the
square porthole in the observer's cockpit canopy.

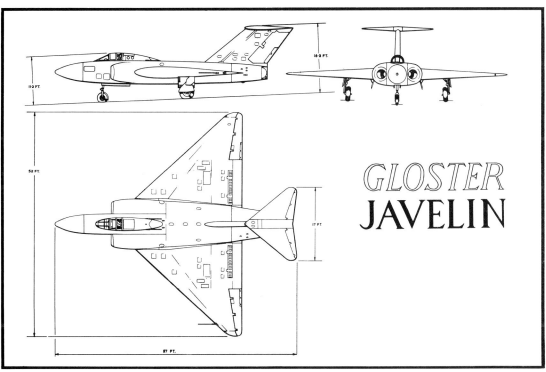

GLOSTER
JAVELIN

2
Proving the Planform

Although Bill Waterton was to state later that the Javelin was 'as easy to fly as an Anson', the first flight was not an unqualified success.

As soon as WD804 had taken-off, severe vibration set in. As the aircraft gathered speed the vibration became worse. After a few minutes Waterton concluded that the trouble was associated with the rudder. This was soon confirmed by the pilot in the accompanying Meteor 'chase' aircraft, who reported that he could clearly see the rudder being buffeted.

Waterton wisely reduced speed, and conducted only a provisional assessment of the general handling of the aircraft before landing 34 minutes later.

The buffeting was quickly diagnosed as being caused by interference between the engine efflux and the airflow over the rear fuselage. The path of the offending airflow was determined easily, because oil leaking from the Sapphires' centre and rear bearings, which were lubricated on the 'total loss' principle, from two vents below the rudder, left visible streaks across its lower surface.

Wind tunnel tests were conducted, together with further flight tests with a wool-tufted rear fuselage to determine the solution. As a result the fairing around the jet pipes was lengthened to line up with the end of the fuselage, thereby assisting the fineness ratio. Three progressive changes were made and on each occasion the buffeting threshold improved by approximately 50kts. However, the problem was not completely cured until the guard rails running parallel to the parachute fairing on top of the tailplane were removed.

With this relatively simple 'fix' the flight test programme resumed, again with Waterton at the controls. Handling characteristics were assessed, manoeuvring tests completed and the maximum speed was gradually pushed higher and higher as the flight envelope was explored and extended.

In March 1952 the extension to the aft fuselage was accompanied by the lengthening of the jet pipes by 2ft. By this time sufficient experience had been gained for the company to prepare a confidential initial assessment of the aircraft's performance and potential.

Serviceability during the three months was described as 'exceptional'; on only one occasion was the aircraft 'pushed back into the hangar when it was scheduled to fly'. this was due to air in the hydraulic brake system. Great credit for this high degree of serviceability was given to the engines, which in spite of developing more power than any others then in production, were proving more reliable than ever before experienced by Glosters on a prototype.

The report acknowledged that the controls were heavy at first, adding that this was to be expected with a new configuration, as it was necessary to ensure no possibility of overbalanced controls. The aileron gear ratio was increased, resulting in a significant improvement. Confidence was expressed in being able to reach

Below: WD804 with its first modification; an interim jet-pipe fairing, one of several shapes tried to solve the tail buffet problem.

Above: WD804 with a further evolved jet-pipe fairing. Visible at the rear is the engine oil vent pipe extensions. The anti-spin tail parachute has been removed.

Left: WD808, the second prototype, taking off for its first flight, on 21 August 1952, from the Gloster test airfield at Moreton Valence.

Below left: A fine 'ground' photograph of the second prototype, WD808.

Left: The distinctive 'pen-nib' jet-pipe fairing finally evolved to solve the tail buffet problem (right) shown alongside the extended rear fuselage and angled jet-pipe nozzles of the Javelin F(AW) Mk 7 (left) with the more powerful Sa7 Sapphire engines.

Right: WT827, the third Javelin prototype, was the first to have a radome and to carry armament. In this view the aircraft has an experimental bull-nose radome.

Below right: Another view of WT827 with the experimental bull-nose radome. Note the opened canopy, which slid back in one piece on the early prototypes. Just visible in the cockpit is Bill Waterton, Gloster Chief test pilot at the time.

the 'magic figure of 210 degrees rate of roll per second produced by Fighter Command as their ideal'.

Flying had been carried out at all altitudes from sea level to 43,000ft, during which both the pressurised aircraft and its Sapphire engines showed 'extreme promise'. A Mach number of 0.915 had been reached in level flight at 60% of full engine power, and 'no indication of reaching the steep portion of the drag rise curve had been detected by pilots'.

Handling qualities cannot be adequately expressed on paper, but the report included the following in order to convey some key points:

'The stalling speed is 73kts with the aircraft flying at 85% of its all-up weight with landing gear and flaps up.

'The landing speed with the aircraft at an angle of attack of 4° in excess of the normal static attitude is under 90kts. The aircraft is pulling up in 500yd without ill-treating the brakes unduly. Using half-flap for take-off at the above weight, the aircraft is unsticking in 300yd with a wind speed below 5mph.'

The report included the story that 'on one occasion our Chief Test Pilot was flying the aircraft in poor visibility and did not see the end of the runway quickly enough to line himself up comfortably for the approach. He had to make a quick turn at the last moment and found himself over the runway with 130kts on the clock and 300ft too high. On this particular occasion he used 1,200yd of runway'.

The report considered this episode 'illustrated most forcibly the characteristics of the aircraft to suit its particular all-weather role with its docility in handling, and exceptional take-off and landing capabilities'.

Phase II of the flight test programme began in April, with the lengthened jet pipes already mentioned, more powerful engines and the tail parachute fairing removed.

During this period the Ministry of Supply began a competitive analysis of the GA5 against the competing de Havilland DH110, which had in fact made its first flight in September 1951, two months before the Gloster aircraft had flown. The rivalry between the two competing companies was intense, the de Havilland test pilots irreverently referring to the Javelin as 'The Trug'. As is customary the Ministerial study considered not only the performance and cost of the aircraft involved, but the wider aspects of available resources, location of manufacturing facilities and the current and future commitments of the companies concerned. In this assessment it seems as if Ministry officials were among other things, very impressed by the development potential of the delta-winged Gloster contender. Flt Lt D. Miller seconded to the Operational Requirements section during this period, recalls that although the DH110 was, at that time, the better aircraft from the performance point of view, it was considered that the swept-wing, twin-boom layout was at the end of its development potential. The Javelin, on the other hand, with its delta-wing planform, represented the beginning of a new era of aerodynamic technology. The possibility of a developed thin-wing Javelin was apparently foreseen at this early stage.

Testing proceeded satisfactorily until 29 June 1952, when disaster struck on the 99th flight. This was intended to investigate the behaviour of the aircraft during runs at low altitude, and during one of these the aircraft suddenly developed elevator flutter, and before Bill Waterton could decelerate both elevators broke away from the tailplane. Control obviously became critical but Waterton used his skill and experience to regain some control in pitch by means of the electrically-operated variable-incidence tailplane.

Although the response was slow due to the difficulty of moving the large trimming wheel, Waterton simulated several 'approaches' and 'landings' at altitude to get the feel of the aircraft before attempting to land on the 10,000ft long runway at the Armament Experimental Establishment's airfield at Boscombe Down.

All went well until the aircraft touched down when the higher than usual speed coupled with a sudden drop caused the landing gear to collapse. The aircraft skidded along the ground for several hundred yards and then caught fire. In spite of some difficulty in opening the canopy, Waterton managed to escape unharmed and, before leaving the blazing wreck, even salvaged some of the auto-observer records. Although the airfield fire service arrived at the scene quickly and soon extinguished the fire, the aircraft was damaged beyond repair.

For his skill in saving the test records and for 'courage beyond the call of duty' Waterton was subsequently awarded the George Medal, Britain's highest award in time of peace.

With the loss of WD804 the flight test programme came to a standstill. In spite of this setback, however, the Ministry of Supply announced on 7 July 1952 that a substantial production order had been placed for the Gloster fighter, bestowing upon it the name Javelin officially.

The aircraft was ordered into 'Super Priority' production, this category having been instituted by Winston Churchill to enable a relatively small number of military types, specially chosen for their importance to the Services re-equipment programme, to obtain the benefit of priority in acquiring materials, proprietary components and manpower.

The decision to afford Javelin production this degree of priority had in fact been taken some time before it was chosen from the two types in competition, for Lord De L'Isle and Dudley (Secretary of State for Air) had told the House of Lords on 3 April 1952, 'The Prime Minister has accorded super-priority to the production of . . . an all weather fighter of a type to be decided shortly'.

Right: Start up, with the cloud of black smoke which this operation characteristically produced. The prototype ladder is noteworthy. This aircraft, XA552, was later fitted with two de Havilland Gyron Junior engines, as part of the programme for the Bristol 188 research aircraft.

Below: Unusual stern view of WT827.

Bottom: WT827, with another experimental radome and a modified canopy embodying a square window above the rear cockpit. The white section of the canopy is a Durestos fairing for the Gee aerial.

Following the loss of the first prototype, work accelerated on the second aircraft WD808 which, fortunately was already well advanced. This aircraft was similar in external appearance to the WD804, complete with an anti-spin parachute on top of the tailplane.

Internally, however, there were many modifications and improvements, the most significant of which was the installation of more powerful ASSa6 Sapphires, each developing 8,200lb static thrust. The aircraft made its first flight on 21 August 1952, with Bill Waterton at the controls just seven weeks after the loss of WD804.

The aircraft was not armed, and displayed on its all metal nose the Hawker Siddeley winged badge in preparation for its public debut which it made a few days later at the SBAC Flying Display at Farnborough.

Because the cause of the crash of WD804 had not been fully investigated and because of its low accumulated flying hours, WD808 performed under severe limitations. Waterton had to restrict his display to low speed, low altitude flying, but nevertheless impressed spectators with his performance.

After Farnborough, the aircraft returned to Moreton Valence for the installation of a flight resonance system, in keeping with modern testing techniques. This was the first time such a system had been fitted to a British aircraft, and, with it installed, flight trials recommenced in January 1953. By this time other Gloster test pilots were contributing to the programme along with Bill Waterton. These included Brian Smith, Geoff Worrall, Peter Lawrence, and the now legendary Jan Zurakowski. Sqn Ldr Peter Scott, the RAF project liaison pilot, also got airborne in WD808.

On 7 March 1953 the third prototype, WT827, was flown by Bill Waterton. Unlike the first two prototypes, which were assembled at the wartime dispersal factory at Bentham, this aircraft was produced at Hucclecote, as were all subsequent Gloster-built Javelins. WT827 was intended primarily for armament trials, and was the first Javelin to carry the four wing-mounted 30mm Aden guns, A1 radar and a nose radome. Apart from this it closely resembled the second prototype. The armament trials were highly successful. The aircraft was also used for generator cooling, general engineering, radome development and flight refuelling trials.

For the refuelling trials, a probe was fitted on the starboard wing, but its location behind the pilot made the actual refuelling operation both difficult and hazardous. Later an improved installation, involving a long lance-like probe mounted on the side of the fuselage and extending beyond the nose, was developed.

During the radome development trials the aircraft was flown through rain and hail, when it was found that the neoprene protective skin on the Hycar radome quickly eroded. Many attempts were made to improve the adhesion, but failed. Success only came when the shape of the radome was modified. Several different shapes were tested. The final type tested was short and bulbous, and with it WT827 made its first public showing, on 15 July, when Bill Waterton made a 575mph flypast over Odiham on the occasion of the Queen's Coronation Review of the Royal Air Force.

The most effective radome, from both the aerodynamic and electronics points of view, was distinctly 'needle' pointed, and this shape was adopted for all production Javelins. Slight variations were made between radomes housing British and American radar.

In March 1953, as part of an evaluation of several European aircraft by the US Air Force under the Mutual Defence Aid Program (MDAP), Col R. Johnson and Col P. Everest visited Glosters to test the Javelin, flying the second prototype. Among several favourable comments made was that it was a 'very stable gun platform'.

The evaluation resulted, 18 months later, in the allocation by the US of some £37million under the MDAP for the procurement of British military aircraft, the great majority of which were Javelins.

In March 1954 Bill Waterton left Glosters, his place as chief test pilot being taken by Wg Cdr R. F. 'Dicky' Martin DFC, AFC, who had joined the company some months previously.

The flight trials of 1952 with the first and earlier wind-tunnel tests had indicated that a fairly minor modification to the wing could be made that would significantly increase the lift at the tips and thereby improve manoeuvrability, at altitude. A sharply swept wing is prone to tip stalling and high subsonic Mach numbers, mainly because of the accentuated span-wise flow.

The modification to the Javelin wing entailed 'kinking' the leading edge to reduce the amount of sweepback from a point approximately half span out to the tip. Sweep on the inboard section of the wing remained at 39.5°, but the sweep outboard was reduced to 33.8°.

This had the effect of increasing the tip chord and reducing the thickness/chord ratio of the wing as a whole. The reduced spanwise airflow not only improved the tip stalling but the lift coefficient as well at high subsonic speeds. In turn this improved the manoeuvrability so desirable in the techniques being evolved for launching air-to-air guided missiles.

The modified wing was fitted first to WD808, the second prototype, other changes included a strengthened tail, to reduce stick forces at high speeds, and the reduction of the elevator control ratio from the original 5 to 1 to 7.4 to 1. Thus modified the aircraft

Left: WT827, the third prototype Javelin, formates with WD808, the second prototype.

Below: WT830, the fourth prototype, displays to advantage the revised wing shape with a kinked leading edge introduced on this aircraft.

Right: WT836, the fifth and last prototype Javelin, with an interim nose radome and twin Perspex canopies for the pilot and navigator.

made the first flight on 28 May 1953. Only two weeks later the prototype was completely destroyed in a crash at Flax Bourton, near Bristol, which also killed the pilot. The accident was in no way attributable to the new wing, which was in fact adopted on all subsequent aircraft.

The crash was particularly tragic because the pilot, Peter Lawrence, deliberately remained in the aircraft to avoid crashing on schoolchildren playing in a field, and finally ejected too low to allow his parachute to open properly.

The aircraft had been engaged in tests with the CG further aft than had been tried previously, and got into a 'super stall' condition. When the auto-observer was recovered from the wreckage it became possible to determine the sequence of events. The descent, from about 11,000ft, took only about 60sec. No airspeed was evident on the trace, indicating that the aircraft descended almost vertically.

The death of Lawrence initiated an intensive investigation, not only into the cause of the accident itself, but also into the whole subject of stalling characteristics at high angles of attack. It was discovered that at very high angles the aircraft entered what is known variously as a 'super-stall', 'deep stall' or 'stable stall'. This condition occurred at speeds of less than 80kts when the very large and powerful flaps were lowered. As the flaps deployed, the nose of the aircraft rose and the condition of 'super-stall' achieved. The aircraft then commenced descending almost vertically, in this condition the tailplane was blanked by the wing, resulting in complete loss of elevator control.

With the cause of the accident diagnosed, Glosters set about finding a solution. In the meantime pilots were warned of the dangers involved once a Javelin enters a 'super-stall' condition, and were instructed to bale out if recovery was not achieved while sufficient altitude remained.

Several cures for the problem were, in fact developed. By installing semi-slatted flaps, the nose-up pitch change condition became much less severe. However, as the basic cause of the trouble was tip stalling which spread rapidly along the wings as the angle of attack increased, attention focused on the leading edges. Wind tunnel tests on models fitted with pronounced drooped leading edges were not promising, but further tests indicated that leading-edge slats were one solution. A trial set of slats was fitted to aircraft XA548 and flown. The slats proved highly successful, but the additional weight, about 400lb, of the 'fix' was considered unacceptable by the Air Ministry.

The solution finally adopted was to fit a stall warning system. This comprised a small metal plate mounted on hinges perpendicular to the upper surface of the wing, near the tip of the mid chord. At the onset of a stall, the plate was sucked forward by the low-pressure generated over the leading-edge. A microswitch contact was then broken, which in turn, set-off a buzzer in the cockpit.

Spinning in a Javelin was, for those unprepared for it, a somewhat frightening experience. Although the rate of rotation was quite slow, the nose of the aircraft pitched through about 70° during each turn. In the spin the Javelin lost height at the high rate of 240ft/sec. 'Dicky' Martin made nearly 200 test spins in order to study the phenomenon and to evolve the recovery technique. This involved the application of into-spin ailerons pushing the stick forward and adjusting the tailplane setting to give a nose-down attitude.

21

A significant contribution to the spinning trials was made by the use of models dropped from a captive balloon. These tests were evolved at Cardington, in conjunction with the RAE, and involved dropping a 6ft scale model which was 'pre-spun' on a turntable beneath the balloon. A number of drops were made, during which small electric motors operated the flying controls, including the flaps, and the model was filmed through its fall. At a pre-determined altitude a parachute was deployed automatically to permit a safe recovery.

At this stage of its development the Javelin was receiving criticism from certain people and quarters which Gloster felt was unjustified.

In particular the criticism concentrated on the capacity of the internal fuel tanks and the maximum speed of the aircraft; both were judged to be inadequate. Mr Woodrow Wyatt, MP for Aston Division, Birmingham, commented in the House of Commons on 1 March 1955 that the Javelin had 'a fuel capacity of only 800 gallons'.

It is not known what this MP thought the capacity should have been. The internal capacity was, in fact 765gal and this was soon supplemented by the installation of two underwing tanks each of 250gal. Because of their appearance and location on the underside of the aircraft, they became known as bosom tanks. These tanks were fitted to WT827, which flew with them for the first time on 4 June 1953.

Criticism regarding the aircraft's speed was dramatically stilled on the evening of 4 July when many thousands of Londoners were startled by a 'bang' from the sky which many recognised as being caused by an aeroplane 'going supersonic'. The bang, in fact, was caused by 'Dicky' Martin in a Javelin.

The incident caused questions to be asked in the House of Commons. In reply to these, Mr Maudling, Economic Secretary to the Treasury, explained in the House, 'The aircraft was cruising at high altitude and near the speed of sound when the pilot's oxygen supply failed; during the ensuing confusion he inadvertently exceeded the speed of sound, causing the bang'.

This was not the first time the Javelin had exceeded Mach 1.0, it had first achieved sonic speed several weeks previously.

Dicky Martin was also at the controls of the fifth and last prototype WT836 when this first took to the air on 20 July 1954. This was very representative of the production Javelin Mark 1, and featured the kinked wing, powered ailerons, elongated radome and much operational equipment.

A major difference from its four predecessors was the cockpit canopy, which was of all-Perspex for both the pilot and the navigator. The top contour of the canopy was also raised slightly, because it was found that under conditions of negative g the new nylon seat harness stretched allowing the crew member to move upwards so that there was insufficient room above his helmet for him to grasp the ejector-seat blind-handle. The new canopy also facilitated the wearing of the new 'bone dome' protective helmets then being introduced into the services.

Below: XA563 and XA564 airborne in 1955 show the short sharp-pointed radomes then in favour. XA564 has a metal nose cone.

On the first four prototypes, the canopy was transparent over the pilot only. The navigator was covered by a single piece metal canopy with only two small circular windows each side. The original theory that the navigator could operate his radar displays better in semi-darkness had been rendered obsolete by the development of the more advanced radars. Also, it was realised that the navigator had other tasks and that these could be performed more efficiently if he had all-round vision. The new type of canopy became standard on all production Javelins.

The fifth prototype was used mainly for engineering trials. These included tests on the new canopy at Boscombe Down, where it was subjected to jettisoning trials in the 'blower' rig. The aircraft was also used for a number of trial installations of equipment.

Only two days after WT836 took to the air, the first production Javelin F(AW)1 flew, with Dicky Martin at the controls. Serial numbered XA544, this was the first of 40 Javelin Mk 1 aircraft to roll off the Hucclecote production lines. Twenty-nine of these were to be delivered to the RAF, but the remaining 11 Javelins were retained and used by Glosters and Ministry Establishments for further trials and development work — an indication of the inadequacy of the number of prototypes ordered by the Ministry for the Javelin programme.

The first production aircraft, XA544, was used for operational checks on armament, instrumentation and other trial installations. XA545 was the first Javelin to embody the all-flying tail unit, XA546 was fitted with a Gee 3 installation, and also used for spinning trials.

XA544 and XA546, together with the three prototypes WT827, 830 and 836, took part in the SBAC Display at Farnborough in September 1954, giving the public the opportunity to compare production and prototype aircraft. Five aeroplanes of the same type is an unusual event at Farnborough and in its coverage of the display *The Aeroplane* reported they provided 'an impressive spectacle, with a paired take-off and fly-past in formation, before an individual aerobatic display by Wg Cdr R. F. Martin'.

The appearance of the Javelin at Farnborough engendered more than normal spectator interest. One group of people, wearing badges giving them access to the generally restricted 'flying areas', were noticed to be taking close-up photographs of the engine air inlets with an intensity not normal for members of the press. Enquiries revealed that the gentlemen in question were in fact members of the Russian embassy. It is understood that they were politely but firmly escorted from the aircraft and their films confiscated.

A foretaste of the Javelin's performance at height was given during a visit to Canada for cold weather trials shortly before it entered service.

At that time it was customary for a Canadian crew from the test site at Namao, Alberta to come to Britain to collect aircraft for such trials. In the case of the

Below: An indication of the intensive nature of the development flying programme in mid 1955 is given by this line up of Javelins at the Gloster test airfield at Moreton Valence. Aircraft XA552, the nearest machine, embodies the latest refinements, including a blunt-tipped radome, twin sliding Perspex canopies and kinked wing leading edge.

Javelin, however, they declined to do so in view of its relatively short range. It was then proposed that the aircraft should be ferried across the Atlantic onboard the carrier HMCS *Magnificent*, after which it would be either flown off when near the coast or disembarked in Nova Scotia and flown North by the RCAF crew. This proposal was also turned down by the RCAF.

At this point, N. F. Penny, a member of the Flight Testing Teams at A&AEE Boscombe Down, was brought into the problem because of his previous trans-Atlantic experience. With his pilot, Sqn Ldr David Dick, an evaluation of the aircraft in question, XA723, was made to determine precisely its capabilities as regards maximum range and optimum cruising altitudes. These evaluations were conducted from Moreton Valence during August 1956. After two weeks it was established that it was quite feasible for the Javelin to cross the Atlantic via Iceland and Greenland.

And so, in September 1956, painted a handsome Day-Glo red, and equipped with twin 'bosom' tanks and, specially for the flight, a Marconi radio compass, the Javelin departed from Moreton Valence. It was accompanied by a Hastings support aircraft from Boscombe Down carrying the ground crew and Engineering Officer. The first leg was to Prestwick, for a night stop prior to the long hop to Keflavick in Iceland.

From Keflavick the Javelin hopped to Narsassauak ('Bluey West 1') in Greenland, and from there to Goose Bay in Labrador. The flights between each point on this trans-Atlantic run were carried out at altitudes varying between 45,000 and 48,000ft the most economical height, and were of relatively short duration. The only problem was that the Javelin had to wait for the Hastings support aircraft to catch it up to permit refuelling with the special coupling that was necessary, and also to have it checked out, and for the ground crew to assist the crew out of and into their heavy immersion suits.

After a night stop in Goose Bay, XA723 departed to an RCAF Night Fighter training unit just out of Quebec where it was demonstrated before onflying to Uplands Ottawa. After a further night stop, on to Namao in Alberta, stopping at one of the Great Lakes airfields for refuelling, where the local bush pilots, male and female, enthused over the aircraft.

The whole journey was conducted trouble free and the aircraft created great interest wherever it put down. Penny recalls, 'I have very vivid memories of the excitement it caused in the air when by radio we announced our approach to Goose Bay from Greenland and the control authorities scrambled a section of F-89 night fighters to intercept us. Being aware of this proposed interception, having intercepted the radio calls, we maintained altitude at 48,000ft and watched

Left: Javelin F(AW) Mk 4, XA630, used for handling trials and flight trials of the fuel system.

Above right: Fine study of Javelin F(AW) Mk 1, XA552, displaying its well-named bosom tanks to advantage. This aircraft was later used as a test bed for the de Havilland Gyron Junior engine, as part of the programme for the Bristol 188 supersonic research aircraft.

Right: Javelin F(AW) Mk 7, XH712, with metal nose fairing and yaw and vane boom for handling trials at Boscombe Down.

with some interest the American aircraft reach their ceilings at something between 43,000 and 45,000ft. Then, in close proximity to the Goose Bay Airfield, we received landing clearance from that altitude and released the most effective air brakes that the Javelin carried, and effected a wing-over vertical descent on the airfield through the middle of the American formation. It proved such an effective manoeuvre that we were on the ground and at the dispersal point before they had actually rejoined circuit for landing'.

This was the only occasion known that the Javelin crossed the Atlantic.

XA546, one of the five aircraft demonstrated at Farnborough, was sadly lost on 21 October when Flt Lt R. J. Ross, an RAF pilot, crashed into the Bristol Channel. During the subsequent enquiry, it was concluded that the pilot was attempting to recover from an intentional spin at too low an altitude, the Javelin's very high rate of descent giving him no time to regain level flight before he hit the water. Sadly, Ross's body was never recovered.

The fourth production Javelin, XA547 was used for initial trials of the de Havilland Firestreak missiles, then code-named 'Blue Jay', and XA548, fitted with an anti-spin parachute, special tail bumper, drooped wing leading-edge and slats for the exacting and time consuming spinning trials. XA561 was also used for spinning, at Boscombe Down. XA549 was used for the development of various types of radio and radar installations.

By the autumn of 1954 the Javelin was attracting the attention of NATO air forces, particularly those which were already operating Meteors. In October, a Belgian evaluation team, headed by Lt-Cols C. Roman and G. de Beuger flew XA546 a short time before it was lost, but in spite of Gloster's initial optimism no export orders materialised.

The Javelin appeared at more shows in 1955, making its debut at Paris in June of that year, when XA556 was displayed by Geoff Worrall. In July XA544 took part in the RAF Golden Jubilee Celebrations at Farnborough, and XA564 and XA565 appeared there at the annual flying display. On the Tuesday of this particular Farnborough Geoff Worrall delighted the crowds by performing the first half of an outside loop or bunt, the first time this manoeuvre had been demonstrated by a Javelin. During the show the Javelin also demonstrated its ability to cope with a sudden engine failure — which it did so successfully that few of the spectators were aware that they had watched a single-engine landing.

Flight trial activity accelerated during 1955. An indication of the valuable contribution made to the programme by the production aircraft involved, is the fact that because of their availability, more test flying hours were accumulated in the last six months of that year than were flown in the three previous years. This also indicates the inadequacy of even the increased number of prototypes finally ordered. The importance of having sufficient aircraft for the development of a modern combat aircraft had been officially recognised in a White Paper on the supply of military aircraft issued in February 1955. This recommended 20, but this hindsight came far too late to benefit the Javelin.

The Javelin came of age with the formal issue of the official CA release on 30 November 1955. For most initial purposes the planform had been proved.

Above: Javelin F(AW) Mk 1, XA547, one of several issued to the College of Aeronautics at Cranfield. This particular aircraft is reported to have been fitted with some degree of dual control.

Right: Javelin F(AW) Mk 1, wet but proud at the 1956 Farnborough Air Display.

26

3

Javelins into Service

After the CA release milestone the first three Javelins in F(AW) Mk 1s XA568, XA570 and XA572 were delivered to the RAF. These flew from Moreton Valence to No 23 MU at Aldergrove, Northern Ireland, on 30 December 1955 for acceptance checks and installation of the AI17 radar.

The first of these was then ferried on 24 February 1956 to No 46 Squadron at Odiham for service flying trials under the command of Wg Cdr F. E. W. Birchfield DFC, an experienced Canadian pilot. The big aircraft was greeted by a large crowd of airmen, who had been awaiting its arrival with some trepidation since September the previous year when it was confirmed that the squadron was to be re-equipped with Javelins.

There was basis for the trepidation: the development flying problems; the restrictions on manoeuvres in the looping plane because of the risk of super stall; the fact that it was the RAF's first purpose-built all-weather interceptor fighter. It was the first twin-jet delta fighter in the world and the Javelin was also by far the heaviest fighter ever to go into service with the RAF — its 31,000lb plus was half as much again as that of the night fighting Meteors it was replacing.

Underlying the trepidation, however, was a genuine feeling of pride throughout the squadron in being chosen as the first one to receive this new potent addition to Britain's defensive capability, in spite of the comments of 'Flat-iron', the 'Jabberwock' and even the 'Beast'. The first aircraft were formally accepted by the RAF on 29 February.

In June tragedy struck the squadron when the Commanding Officer, Birchfield, and his navigator became the first in-service Javelin casualties when their aircraft crashed while returning to Odiham in bad weather at night. He was succeeded by Wg Cdr H. E. White DFC, AFC, under whom the squadron embarked upon the intensive phase of the flying trials.

The intensive flying programme entailed reaching 1,000 flying hours as quickly as possible. To achieve this, pairs of Javelins took off at 30-minute intervals from 8.30 in the morning to 2.30 in the afternoon, and again from 6.30 in the evening until night flying ceased at 2.30 the following morning, practising every operational procedure until, within eight weeks, the total was reached.

As might be expected with a new aircraft, there were the usual crop of teething troubles, but the attention paid to 'maintenance' during the design stage was appreciated by the ground crews. Initially, access to the cockpit was by way of a footrest and handhold at the rear end of the left side. This necessitated a long slippery walk up the wing and fuselage, but Glosters developed a 'direct access' curved ladder which fitted over the left air intake. This eased access to the cockpit, but the ground crews did not appreciate the weight of the rather hefty ladder or its location pins, which had to be inserted in holes hidden by the curvature of the intake. 'Holing in one' needed quite a bit of practice, especially at night in windy weather. The heavy ladder was in marked contrast to the light-weight steps developed for the Venom and Hunter, and resulted in some people referring to one Javelin unit as the 'Bomber Squadron'.

In spite of its novel configuration, the Javelin proved an easy aeroplane to fly. However, at this early stage there was no dual-control version available and so two pilots were sent to Boscombe Down where they received initial conversion training from the Handling Squadron. On their return to Odiham they in turn trained other pilots. As an introduction to the aircraft, each pilot was given a ride in the rear cockpit by one of the qualified pilots. During this ride the pilot was introduced to the stalling characteristics, the effects of the air brakes (startling!) and a run down on circuit procedures. The first solo normally followed at short notice, each pilot flying with his navigator on this and subsequent flights.

The airbrakes were a distinctive feature of Javelin flying. They were infinitely variable, rapid in their action and extremely powerful, all of which made them a useful aid in a variety of circumstances, including close combat. Indeed, such was their sensitivity that, paradoxically, they could be used to save fuel. If a 'battle' formation of four aircraft was returning to base a little short of fuel, they would remain at height (where fuel consumption was significantly lower) until the last possible moment. The leader would then order

'half airbrake' and close his throttles completely. The other aircraft, also on fully-closed throttles, could hold station by judicious adjustment of airbrake and, if the leader judged the ensuing rapid descent with skill, the whole formation could arrive in the circuit with virtually no discernible reduction in fuel state from the start of the manoeuvre. The airbrake system also included a limiter which prevented their full extension above 430kts to protect the airframe. If full airbrake extension was selected above this speed, the surfaces only partially deployed until this speed was reached. The airbrakes then snapped open fully, producing a violent 1g deceleration.

The Javelin flying syllabus comprised seven flights as follows:

Flight 1 — first solo. Starting up procedures were followed by brake familiarisation. Since many pilots had no experience of hydraulically-operated toe brakes, some taxying practice was essential. Flight No 1 continued with take-off, climb to 30,000ft, turns and the use of variable air brakes. The pilot then descended to 5,000ft, followed by a high speed run, deceleration, an overshoot, and landing.

Flight 2. This was an exercise in manual control. Flying with the rudder and elevators in manual presented no problem, provided the aircraft was correctly trimmed. With bad trimming the stick loads were very heavy. The flight ended with a controlled descent and a Ground Controlled Approach landing.

Flight 3. After a full power climb to 40,000ft the aircraft was accelerated in level flight to the onset of the compressibility buffet. This was gentle and easily recognised. A succession of high-speed turns up to the stall threshold followed, the flight ending with a let-down and a Ground Controlled Approach.

Flight 4. Further practice in hard steep turns, at high Mach numbers, above 40,000ft. Descent to 5,000ft was made with full airbrakes and the throttles closed. Flg Off E. Wright, ARAeS, a pilot of No 46 Squadron, described this as a 'startling manoeuvre', with the aeroplane going down almost vertically, but very steadily, at Mach 0.90. Tight turns at high speeds were made at the lower level.

Flight 5. This introduced pilots to flight on asymmetric power. On the Javelin this presented no problem at all, due partly to the toe-in of the inset engines and partly to the excellent trim and power assisted rudder. The safety speed was very low, 120kts, and was actually attained before unsticking. The flight included re-lighting the engines, and an approach and overshoot in manual.

Flight 6. This simulated a high-level interception at long range, enabling crews to assess fuel consumption under operational conditions. An outstanding characteristic of the Javelin was its fuel economy on let-down, which of course benefited its performance in the interception area. Pilots could begin a glide let-down at high altitude and extreme range, and enter the circuit having used a remarkably small amount of fuel.

Flight 7. This was a repeat of Flight No 6, but at night. The forward vision from the front cockpit was excellent for night flying, although, in common with many of its contemporaries, the vision deteriorated rapidly in heavy rain. This was cured on the Mk 7 and later aircraft by a hot air blast system.

It took about six weeks to convert all of the squadron crews. This was slightly longer than that anticipated, because of unserviceability among the few aircraft then delivered. Generally, however, the between sorties turn-round time was much shorter than with the

Meteor. This was due mainly to the fact that the various equipment bays were generally more accessible and to the provision of the pressure-refuelling points under the wing roots. Engine starts were also quicker, being actioned by cartridges which when fired produced not only clouds of dense black smoke from the exhaust ports under the fuselage, but a shrill hissing noise.

However, the sound which became to be associated with the Javelin was not that of the starter cartridges, but the very distinctive and to some people disagreeable booming or 'mooing' whine generated by the

Left: Javelin F(AW) Mk 1s.

Below: Javelin F(AW) Mk 1s of No 46 Squadron.

Right: Entry into the cockpit was eased by the development of this ladder. Previously the crew had to climb over the trailing edge and walk up the slippery wing.

Above: Javelin F(AW) Mk 1, being piloted by Sqn Ldr H. G. James AFC, DFM, Commander of E Flight with No 46 Squadron, as he achieved his 6,000th flying hour.——

Right: An echelon of Javelin F(AW) Mk 1s of No 46 Squadron.

Below right: The four Javelins in the photograph begin to peel away, displaying the massive delta wing to advantage. The Squadron marking, a red arrowhead, was sometimes applied to the fin and sometimes to the nose.

30

Sapphire engines when at idling speed. When airborne, the engine noise together with that caused by the air flowing over the gun ports, made the 'Javelin sound', resulting in the nickname by one unknown comedian of 'harmonious dragmaster'.

The starter cartridges were the source of several of the Javelin's more serious in-service teething troubles. When a cartridge fired, cordite gas was generated which was fed to the turbine starter which engaged the engine, spinning it to 2,000rpm when it was designed to disengage. Sometimes, however, the starter failed to disengage, when it usually disintegrated violently within a few seconds as the engine drove it at unacceptable speeds. The explosions on such occasions were severe, piece of metal scarring both the ground and the underside of the aircraft. There were arguments as to who were most alarmed by such incidents, the crew on board the aircraft, or the ground crew near it!

Pilot problems were relatively few as, already mentioned, the Javelin was an easy aeroplane to fly. A few old habits died hard. One such habit was exhibited by some pilots converting from Meteor Mks 12 and 14. These aircraft were steered on the ground by means of wheelbrakes which were applied by a hand lever on the control column, differential control being obtained by simultaneous extension of the rudder pedals in the appropriate direction. The Javelin, on the other hand, had toe-operated brakes, steering being effected by depressing the appropriate pedal the required amount. The system was fine until a pilot instinctively applied the Meteor technique. More than one pilot left the perimeter track because of this, including the commanding officer of one flight, much

to the inner delight of his pilots. This problem was overcome by the definite introduction of taxying practice.

More serious was the reluctance of some older ex-Meteor aircrew to 'accept' the ejection seats on the Javelin to the extent that they refused even to remove the seat safety locking pins and flew with them in. This particular problem was resolved by a direct order from the commanding officer concerned that they were to be removed before take-off.

One feature of the Javelin particularly appreciated by ex-Mosquito pilots, was the rapidity with which the safety speed of 120kts was attained before unsticking. This contrasted with the seemingly endless period of about one minute after take-off before the Mosquito reached its safety speed.

Most critical of the Javelin during this early period perhaps, were former Hunter pilots who disliked its lack of clearance for aerobatics in the looping plane even more than the ex-Meteor and Vampire pilots, although the 'ban' by no means meant that pilots never indulged in them. All however, agreed that it was an 'easy' aircraft to fly, forgiving and robust.

The pilots and navigators of No 46 Squadron were not in fact the first Royal Air Force crews to operate the Javelin. Other crews had done so the previous

October during Britain's annual air defence exercise named Exercise 'Beware'.

During this war game two Javelin F(AW)1s were flown from RAF Coltishall, Norfolk, by Wg Cdr E. O. Crew with Sqn Ldr J. Walton, Wg Cdr Dicky Martin with Flt Lt Williamson, and Sqn Ldr P. Scott with Flt Lt Robert J. Jeffries as his navigator/radar operator. Although flown by RAF personnel, the two aircraft involved, XA554 and XA559, were not actually Royal Air Force machines, as they were still 'owned' by the Ministry of Supply.

The exercise was a good portent of the Javelin's operational capabilities, which delighted everyone, except one hopes the Russians, by intercepting and claiming the destruction of Canberras over 100 miles out from the coast and even 'jumping' several stray USAF F-100 Super Sabres on the way. At the end of the exercise the aircraft flown by E. O. Crew and J. Walton proudly claimed eight 'kills', this being traditionally symbolised by the painting of eight Canberra bombers in white on the side of the cockpit.

An interesting innovation during the initial entry of the Javelin into service was the establishment as part of No 228 Operation Conversion Unit (OCU) at Leeming of the Javelin Mobile Training Unit (JMTU). Under the command of Sqn Ldr P. D. C. Street DSC, this comprised a specialised team made up of two

Javelin pilots, four navigators, two Valetta pilots and 16 ground crew, the task of which was to assist squadrons in converting to the new fighter. As its name implies, it was continually on the move, both within Britain and in Germany, particularly during the first 12 months when several squadrons were being re-equipped.

The JMTU 'classroom' consisted of Valetta C1s and T4s which were coming into service at the OCU. Usually two Valettas were used in a conversion programme, a T4 and a C1, which was used to transport the ground crew. The JMTU was sent to the base of the squadron concerned before the arrival of its Javelins, and the course began with an in-depth indoctrination, the introductory technical lectures often being given by civilian technicians from Glosters. The aircrew then spent three periods in a simple cockpit simulator, which did not reproduce any flying conditions, being used only to familiarise crews with the cockpit layout, check list drills and emergency procedures. By present day standards it was a crude affair, but at the time it was a useful and effective training aid. The pilots made six day sorties and one at night to complete the conversion.

Navigator training differed. These flew several 'missions' in the Valetta T4, which, equipped with AI17 radar in an extended nose, acted as the 'interceptor', while the C1 took on the role of the 'target' aircraft.

The use of Valettas for training navigators was a big step forward as several interceptions could be made during each flight. Thirteen actual sorties in a Javelin followed the Valetta flights before the navigator conversion was completed.

The first squadrons assisted by the Unit were Nos 23 and 141 at Horsham-St Faith, in February 1957. Of interest is the fact that the JMTU had no Javelins of its own, and the two Unit pilots got in their hours on the type by picking up aircraft at the MUs and flying them to the units concerned. During the flight they worked in a test or two, and after delivery helped with the acceptance checks and gave demonstration flights, but they did little tactical flying.

By January 1958 most of the squadron conversions to the early marks of Javelin had been completed and the Unit returned to Leeming, where it came under the command of Sqn Ldr Mike 'Dusty' Miller in February, to retrain on the later Javelin series, including the Mk 7 with its uprated Sapphires and fully-powered flying controls.

The unit recommenced work in July 1958, when No 33 Squadron received the first Javelin 7. No 64 Squadron at Duxford followed, and by the end of July the following year all the remaining Meteor squadrons had been converted and the Unit was disbanded. During its existence no squadron undergoing conversion ever 'bent' an aircraft, a fact which not only

fully justified the establishment of the unit, but also reflects credit on the flying qualities of the Javelin.

Most aircraft of any standing seem to generate stories, both true and false, and those concerning the Javelin began to germinate early in its career. One such story has been recalled by M. P. Kilburn, who was with de Havilland UK at the time and is now Regional Sales Manager, Europe, for the de Havilland Aircraft of Canada Limited. He recounts 'I managed to wangle a flight in a Javelin in February 1957, to deliver XA702 from Armstrong Whitworth at Bitteswell to RAF Kemble. The flight lasted 50min because I took the opportunity to do a "little handling" on the way. I managed to go supersonic on the third attempt in a dive over the Bristol Channel. The problem was that at high Mach numbers, the Javelin seemed directionally unstable and required some rapid corrections on the rudder to keep it pointing in the right direction'.

Kilburn continues his reminiscence with 'I was later told that at the Aberporth range where models of various fighters had been boosted by rocket to Mach numbers of around three, that a model of the Javelin had turned around at about Mach 1.5 and had then been perfectly stable at well in excess of that figure while flying backwards. I was not surprised after the experience on my one and only flight'.

4
The Javelin Described

In spite of the unorthodox aerodynamics, combining a delta wing with a tailplane of similar planform mounted on top of a large fin, the Javelin structure was quite conventional. Aluminium alloys were used almost exclusively except for a few edging members which were steel. It was extremely robust and was divided into a number of sub-assemblies, to facilitate sub-contract manufacture.

The fuselage was built up from four such assemblies, the largest of these being the front and centre fuselage which were permanently joined during manufacture. The centre fuselage was a highly redundant structure because of the complex load carrying duties it had to perform, and consisted of a main spar frame, a centre structure and six frame-skin-stringer sections.

The main spar frame was the most important single member of the fuselage, and embodied fork-end fittings, which connected on each side with the top and bottom booms of the wing main spar. The spar frame was heavily reinforced at the centre by vertical members to which were attached the box beam centre structure, or keel member, which ran at full depth down the whole centre fuselage. The keel box contained the fin attachments and the wing rear attachment.

Frame-skin-stringer sections were attached to each side of the keel member in three panels to form the engine bays, the lower segments incorporating runners for installation of the engines from the rear. The engine air intakes were built separately and attached to the fuselage sides, and contained the ducts leading to the engine compressor casings.

The front fuselage, which mounted the nose landing gear, included the pressurised cockpits which comprised a thick inner shell, sealed at the front and rear by solid bulkheads and enclosed by an armoured windscreen and the electrically-operated sliding canopy. Cockpit flooring and skin was in heavy gauge light alloy, to give armour protection to the crew in addition to armour plating on the front frame.

The rear fuselage comprised a light semi-monocoque structure, incorporating the engine jet pipe outlet fairings, and was attached to the centre fuselage by toggle action, quick-release fasteners.

At the fuselage nose was the AI radar bay, enclosed by the Hycar radome. On Javelin F(AW) Mks 2, 6

Below: The first production Javelin F(AW) Mk 1, XA544, being photographed and inspected by representatives of the press.

and 8, with US-built radar, the radome was larger and could be pulled forward on special hinges and swung to one side.

A large servicing bay was located below the rear cockpit and between the air ducts. It housed the engine starting equipment, auxiliary gearbox, hydraulic panel, generator control, electrical distribution panel and some radio equipment. Access to the bay was through a large panel in the fuselage bottom skin.

The fin was a two-spar structure, with nose riblets and inter-spar ribs of reinforced light alloy pressings. The root rib was reinforced by extruded channel sections. Plates and Z-section members at the top of each fin spar formed attachments for the small fixed portion of the tailplane.

The tailplane structure consisted of an unswept central tubular spar, of about one third of the span on the hinge line which continued outboard to the tips by

a swept box spar on each side. The rear edge of the torsion box was formed by the elevator shrouds.

The self-stiffening characteristic of the delta planform enabled the Javelin wings to be particularly efficient and relatively simple structures, mounted at three points. The necessary torsion-boxes were formed by the main spars of each wing together with the leading-edge ribs and nose skin. The inboard section of each wing was built as a sub-assembly and contained the fuel tanks, the main landing gear, flaps, airbrakes,

and the gun and ammunition bays. It was joined during manufacture to the outboard panels which carried the Servodyne aileron-control units and the mass-balanced ailerons.

The panels formed complete sub-assemblies and were attached to the inner wings by two fish-plates which tied across the join to take full compression and torsion loads. There was no butt-facing of shear webs and there was no joint between the webs. Shear was taken by a projecting jointing member. On final assembly a riveted joint was made to complete the torsion box and to take some shear.

Primary member of the complete wing was the root rib, as it transferred much of the bending moment loading across the fuselage through the main spar frame. The root ribs and main spar frame together formed the wing bending system which withstood the major flight loads due to lift.

An indication of the efficiency of the Javelin structure is that the prototype wings failed at 114% ultimate design load and the fuselage at 118%. During subsequent testing of a production airframe, at greatly increased aircraft weight, failure occurred at 115% ultimate loading.

Because of the tailplane, unusual on delta-winged aircraft, the Javelin had conventional flying controls; that is ailerons, elevators, a rudder and flaps, all operated from conventional cockpit controls. Large slotted-plate type air brakes were located on the top and bottom surfaces of the inner wing panels in front of the trailing edge. Their use was limited to speed up to 430kts.

Initially, operation of the primary flight controls was power assisted by hydraulic control units having a boost ratio of 5:1 for the ailerons and elevators, and

7.4:1 for the rudder. A proportion of the aerodynamic loads on these surfaces was transmitted back to the control column to give 'feel' to the pilot. Fully-powered ailerons with an hydraulic Q-feel simulator were adopted on the fourth and subsequent aircraft.

All the prototypes, most of the Javelin 1s and some Javelin 2s had an electrically-operated variable-incidence tailplane, but all later marks of aircraft had an hydraulically-operated 'all-flying' tail in which the electric motor was replaced by a screwjack driven by two hydraulic motors. In this system the elevators acted as anti-balance tabs, and twin simulators in the control circuit induced a load proportional to the indicated airspeed.

Two Bristol Siddeley Series 200 Sapphire engines powered the Javelin Mks 7, 8 and 9. The Series 200 was a development of the Series 100 powering earlier Marks, with a flared turbine annulus, achieved by changes in the turbine root and tip diameters. The ASSa7, fitted to the Mk 7, was type-tested in September 1954, at 10,200lb thrust, thus becoming the first British turbojet to be type-tested at over 10,000lb. Production engines were rated at 11,000lb thrust.

The ASSa7LR, fitted to the Mks 8 and 9, was similar to the ASSa7, but with 12% reheat designed for thrust augmentation at heights above 20,000ft.

The Sapphire engine featured an annular air intake, a 13-stage axial flow compressor, a single, annular-type combustion chamber with two high energy igniter plugs, and a two-stage axial turbine. The jet pipe was normally fixed, but a variable nozzle was fitted to the after-burning or re-heat engines.

The location of the engines close to the fuselage centre-line meant that single-engined performance did not present any problems, as all asymmetric rudder

loads were readily trimmed out. The main restriction during service flying was the ban on aerobatic manoeuvres in the looping plane. This limitation was imposed as a safety precaution because of the extreme trim changes as the air speed reduced in the vertical plane during the pull-up, and the subsequent danger of the aircraft getting into a 'deep' or 'stable-stall' attitude. Warning of an impending stall was conveyed to the pilot by a loud buzz in his earphones.

Most important of the Javelin's systems was the hydraulic installation. This powered the flying controls, landing gear, airbrakes, wheel brakes, nose wheel shimmy damper and the oleo leg recuperators.

Three integral pumps, driven by the auxiliary gearbox, provided the 3,000lb/sq in pressure required. One pump supplied the general services, such as the landing gear, flaps and airbrakes, while the other two served the duplicated systems for the flying control power units.

The hydraulic fluid was contained in a two-compartment tank, the system being so arranged that a failure in either compartment or its associated services, would not lead to failure of the powered ailerons. Three hydraulic accumulators were fitted to smooth out any pressure fluctuations and to give immediate operation of the hydraulic services.

The nose and main landing gear units were fitted with Dowty liquid-spring shock absorbers which were topped up automatically in flight from the aircraft hydraulic system. Dunlop disc brakes, controlled by Maxaret anti-skid units, were fitted to the main wheels. The nose wheel castored and was fitted with a self-centring device. Because it had no brake, a small spring-loaded pad was fitted in the nose wheel housing so that it contacted the tyre and stopped the wheel

rotating after it had retracted into the fuselage.

Electrical power was provided by two generators, each having an output of 6,000W, and supplied dc current for the whole electrical system as well as charging the battery. Where necessary, the current was converted to ac to supply the flight instruments, Gee and other radar equipment.

A particularly successful sub-system was the windscreen rain dispersal for bad weather flying. A large quantity of high speed air was fed to a slot at the base of the windscreen and spread over it by the main airflow. The feature was especially valuable during take off, approach and landing. A barometric control inhibited its operation above a certain height.

By contrast, the engine starting system was one of the less successful Javelin features. On the Javelin Mks 1 to 7 the system utilised two big 5in diameter 'howitzer-shell' like cartridges for each engine, one being a reserve. When a cartridge was fired, the expanding cordite gas was fed to the turbine starter which spun the engine until it reached a speed of 2,000rpm, when it was designed to disengage. Unfortunately, it had a marked tendency not to do so, whereupon it overspeeded and disintegrated, causing serious damage to both the metal of the airframe and to the morale of the ground crews.

Other starting problems included failure of the main feed pipe to the starter, failure of the starter motor itself, failure of a cartridge to fire and the simultaneous firing of both the primary and reserve cartridges.

A new liquid-fuel engine starting system was introduced on the Mks 8 and 9, in order to maintain the ability of very rapid engine starts with the greater mass of the Sapphire Sa7R engines of these aircraft. This new system utilised a relatively small cordite cartridge to ignite the rocket-repellent like liquid fuel in a reaction chamber forming part of the turbo starter. The resulting gas generated increased pressure which was fed to the starter turbine. Three cartridges were provided.

The new system was not an unqualified success, proving troublesome initially and throughout its service life. Sometimes — too often according to the ground and air crews concerned — all three cartridges would fail to fire. They were then replaced by three new cartridges. If these also failed to fire, the crews had to wait one hour before a third set could be fitted.

The cartridges were located in the servicing bay behind the rear cockpit, and because of the troubles experienced with the system, the bay hatch was usually left off in case one of the cartridges blew a safety disc, in which case it had to be replaced, or worse, started a fire. The latter could be even more spectacular than those caused by the old big cartridges. One ground engineer recalls that this excessive use of the servicing bay hatch then caused trouble — after a few weeks the screw fasteners began to loosen!

With hindsight, it is fair comment that a relaxation of the Airstaff insistence on a very rapid start capability would have saved many grey hairs — and not a few Javelins.

Although the Sapphire as an engine proved very reliable in service, two engine installation problems caused concern and loss of aircraft.

The most serious problem was that of compressor blade vibration which arose when Javelins began to be

used extensively on the low level role during the Indonesian 'Confrontation' activities against Malaysia. Several machines were lost as a direct result of this problem, which usually resulted in an uncontained failure of the engine, followed by fire. Special test flights established that a resonant frequency existed in the rpm band of 70 to 80%. Further testing indicated that the problem could have been solved by adjustments to the final nozzle area. Before any firm action could be taken, however, the Javelin was withdrawn from RAF service and the test programme was terminated.

The second major engine problem, which also occurred mainly in the Far East, was known as 'centre-line closure'. This happened when flying at maximum power in tropical rain storms. At full power, the blades of the Sapphire compressor would be at maximum stretch with the minimum of blade clearance. When super-cooled water was injected, the compressor housing contracted, causing the blades to contact the housing with catastrophic results. The Air Ministry were aware of this possibility following an incident recorded by the US Air Force with their B-57 'Canberras' with licence-built Sapphire engines. Because the engine on that aircraft produced power surplus to the maximum airframe limitations, they simply cropped the blades with very little loss of maximum power. It was, however, apparently not financially viable to apply this remedy to the engines in the Javelin, due to the then expected short life of the aircraft. When the life was extended, the problem was 'solved' by the addition of abrasive pads inside the casing. When the blade tips contacted these, the tips merely abraded away without catastrophic results.

For its time, the Javelin was well engineered for day-to-day servicing. Noteworthy were the engine bay rails, which made engine replacement much easier than it was on many of its contemporaries — and is on some current aircraft.

The fuselage wings and tail surfaces were liberally provided with access panels and the provision of numerous bays separated the trades of electrics and hydraulics. These facilities, however, by no means solved all the servicing problems. Sgt Mike Stiles, who served with No 23 Squadron for three years, recalls that 'contortionist abilities were needed to gain access to certain stall warning system components' and that 'six-foot rubber arms' were needed to remove the jet pipe thermocouples. Dropping a spanner during the replacement of the upper thermocouples necessitated the removal of an engine to retrieve it; thus the spanners were always secured to the mechanic's wrist by string! A recurring problem was faulty fuel tank contents gauging. The sensors in the system were particularly allergic to water, and the cure for certain tanks if so contaminated was 'to transport the tank sensing units to the cookhouse and bake them in an oven'. This cured the problem nine times out of ten, and was considered worthwhile in spite of the extraordinary number of panel screws which had to be removed to gain access to the tank units. On No 23 Squadron serviceability was good, on several occasions all the aircraft on charge being available for duty.

Top left: Javelin F(AW) Mk 4, XA766, introduced an all-moving tailplane, with the elevators acting as anti-balancing tabs.

Centre left: Javelin F(AW) Mk 6, XA836, taking-off from Hucclecote with test pilot G. Worrall at the controls.

Left: Javelin XH966, the first F(AW) Mk 8, the final production version of the fighter. This version was powered by two Sapphire Sa7R engines, with a limited reheat capability

Right: The special jet pipe reheat nozzle developed for the F(AW) Mk 8 Javelins. Each nozzle embodied 27 inter-leaved segments.

5

Javelins for Jousting

A wide variety of armament was considered during the initial development stages of the Javelin to equip the fighter for jousting.

The Meteor-like P228, proposed to meet Specification F44/46, was armed with four 30mm cannon. The delta-winged P234, meeting Specification F43/46, carried a single 40mm gun mounted under the fuselage.

An unusual alternative to conventional cannon considered was a novel recoilless gun. This weapon, then under development at the Royal Armament Research and Development Establishment Fort Halstead, was halfway between a shell-firing cannon and a rocket projector. A major problem in the installation of large calibre guns in aircraft is not so much the basic weight of such weapons, but the effect of their recoil forces when fired on the flying characteristics of the aircraft concerned. The Halstead gun was basically a tube from which a large anti-aircraft shell was fired forward, while simultaneously a counterbalancing force was provided by the rearward thrust of the escaping propellant gas so that there was little or no recoil reaction on the airframe.

Two versions of the Halstead weapon were proposed. One was basically a 4.5in diameter tube, weighing about 500lb, firing a single 50lb round. The potential destructive power of such a heavy projectile was obvious, but without benefit of any in-flight guidance it required 100% accuracy in aiming, which was not considered likely under combat conditions.

To overcome the limited ammunition problem, it is recorded that a version was proposed with a conventional-breech loading weapon type hopper-feed holding seven rounds, and another one with a large revolver-type magazine. The latter was described as being some 2ft 6in in diameter by 5ft long, and was partly housed in a blister on the underside of the fuselage.

The P248, submitted to meet Specification F43/46 in August 1947, had a single recoilless gun mounted in the centre of the fuselage. The P272, for the F4/48 night fighter, and the P275 for the F3/48, were presented with either four 30mm cannon or four 4.5in recoilless guns in the wings. In the event, the

Below: Gloster Drawing P272, issued on 26 February 1948, shows the F4/48 armed with either four 4½in 'gun tubes' or four 30mm cannon. Note that the 'recoilless' gun tubes, in the port wing, extend the full wing chord.

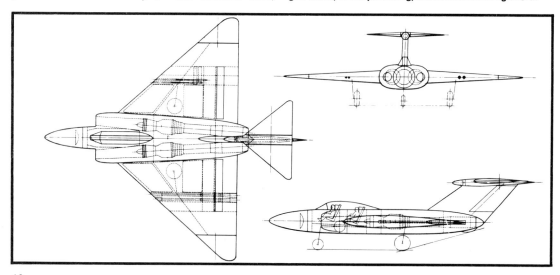

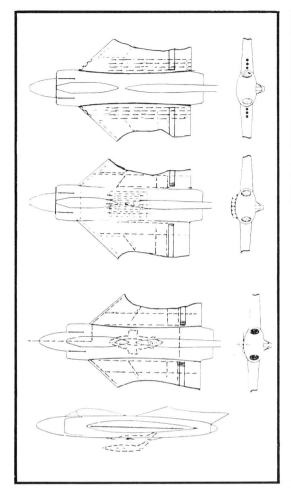

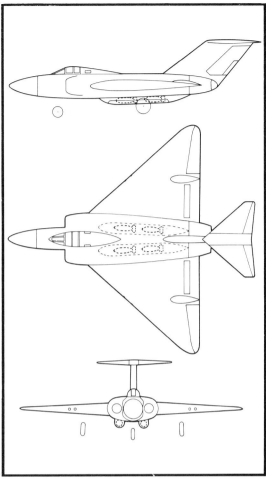

'gun-tube' weapon was not developed to the operational stage.

Other armament considered is shown on P258, prepared in October 1947. This includes a six-rocket projectile battery carried internally in the wing roots, and externally under the fuselage. The drawing also shows a semi-retractable guided missile.

Ultimately, the recoilless gun, rockets and guided missile were discarded in favour of four 30mm Aden guns. The Aden gun was developed from the German MG213C after World War 2 under a programme initiated by the Ministry of Supply at the Armament and Development Establishment at Enfield, hence the name of the weapon. The German MG213C gun was a gas-operated, belt-fed, electrically-fired, pneumatically-charged weapon. By changing certain parts, it could be converted from a 20mm to a 30mm weapon; by reversing certain components, it could be changed from left-hand to right-hand feed.

Above left: Heavy armament was always a major requirement for the Javelin because of its anti-nuclear bomber role. This Gloster drawing, dated October 1947, shows a six-rocket projectile battery carried either internally or externally, and a semi-retractable guided missile.

Above: P317 — drawing issued in May 1950, showing how the F4/48 could be developed to carry four 1,000lb bombs in two streamlined fairings beneath the fuselage. Although the Javelin was used extensively for low level duties, it was in fact never fitted with bombs.

The distinguishing feature of the gun was its revolving drum containing five cartridge chambers parallel to its axis of rotation, and mounted on a shaft within a housing so that each chamber was brought into alignment with the bore of the barrel when it reached the 12 o'clock position during drum rotation. The first successful prototype of the gun was constructed by the

Above: WT827, the third prototype, was used for the initial cannon armament trials.

Right: Javelin F(AW) Mk 4, XA764, on display at the 1956 Farnborough Air Show. The ports for the 30mm Aden cannon are clearly visible in the leading edge.

Far right, top: Early drawing, dated April 1954, showing the Javelin Mks 1 and 2 armed with four Blue Jays, the early code-name for the de Havilland Firestreak.

Far right, bottom: Dummy Firestreak installation and rocket pod on XH758.

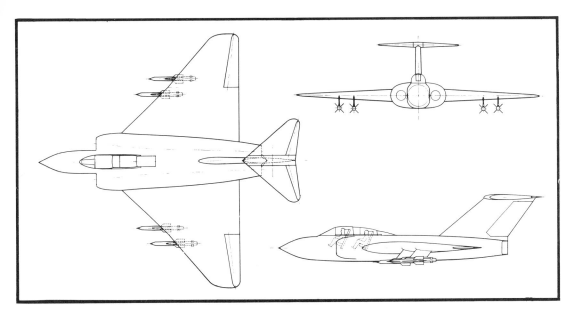

Mauser Works in 1943, but by the time Germany was overrun by the Allies in 1945, only five models to the final design had been completed.

The Aden gun had a rate of fire of about 1,200 rounds a minute, could fire 150 rounds in a continuous burst without overheating, and a special process used in polishing the bore greatly improved barrel life. The Javelin installation brought to bear about eight times more explosive on a target than the previous British standard armament of 20mm Hispano cannon.

The installation of the Aden guns in the thick wing of the Javelin proved easy and relatively trouble free. Each pair of guns was heated by air tapped from the adjacent engine compressor casing. Due to the presence of waste gases in the gun bays when the guns were firing, it was necessary to arrange for a large flow

of air to scavenge these gases. The heating air was used for this. The cannon were first fitted to the third prototype, WT827. Flight trials showed the installation introduced yet another unusual noise adding to the characteristic whine of the Sapphire engines. More serious was the unexpected phenomenon of high induced temperatures of the ammunition which overheated while it remained in the magazines. It was thought that the high temperatures were due to small vortices entering the gun barrels and proceeding down to the ammunition, the interference flow resulting in the magazines becoming heat sinks.

To resolve this problem plastic covers were fitted to the gun muzzles, but these soon melted; measurements showed that, after less than 10 minutes flight, the muzzles reached a temperature of no less than 124°C!

Above left: Javelin F(AW) Mk 4, XH632, shown here at Farnborough, September 1957, was used for development of the Firestreak installation.

Left: Javelin F(AW) Mk 9R, XH707, of No 23 Squadron launches a live Firestreak, during a training mission from the Fighter Command Missile Practice Camp, at Valley, on Anglesey.

Top: Firestreak photographed a split second after it explodes near a Sabre drone.

Above: A live Firestreak about to destroy its drone target. Although no Javelin ever launched a Firestreak in anger, it was an efficient and reliable weapon.

The cure for the problem was found by trying out different lengths of gun barrel protruding from the wing leading edge. The minimum temperatures were obtained using a muzzle which projected 0.25in.

In addition to 'gun' armament, some thought was given to the carriage of bombs. In May, 1950, proposal P317 was prepared showing how the F4/48 could be developed to carry four 1,000lb bombs. These were mounted externally, under the fuselage, in two long streamlined containers. This was only an initial proposal and the idea did not proceed further;

the Javelin was essentially a high-altitude weapon, not a fighter-bomber.

The standard armament of four 30mm Aden cannon which were fitted to Javelin Mks 1, 2, 4, 5 and 6 was only an 'interim' installation. Guided missiles were always envisaged as the ultimate weapons for the Javelin. The missile chosen was the de Havilland weapon originally known by the code-name 'Blue Jay', but later called Firestreak.

The Javelin missile installation involved not only advanced technology as far as the airframe was concerned, but also required the evolution of new operational tactics. Basically, the airframe/missile combination represented a two-stage missile, the Javelin itself being stage 1 and the missile stage 2. As far as the missile was concerned, this embodied an infra-red seeking guidance system which could only 'see' jet engines from the rear, so that a 'pursuit' course was necessary for a successful interception.

The missiles were carried on four pylons under the wings and the development of these involved some clever applied aerodynamics. The location of the pylons under the outer wing panels was tricky because of the high local Mach numbers in the region. It was important that the drag rise was kept as low as possible in order to minimise any reduction in the aircraft's maximum speed or its range.

The pylons swept back from the missiles to the underside of the wings in side elevation. In end-elevation the shape was more sophisticated, because Kuchemann 'waisting' was used. The pylons had a thickness-to-chord ratio of 10%, at top and bottom, reducing to a constant 6% over the centre portion. In addition, the chordwise position of the maximum thickness moved back progressively from the bottom to the top as a means of sweeping back the higher suction isobars.

The final design was very successful in maintaining the top speed with four Firestreaks very close to that of the aircraft in the 'clean' condition, and the reduction in range was minimal.

The trial installation of dummy Firestreaks was made on Javelin Mk F(AW)4, XA632, and what was to be a lengthy programme of development flying began in July 1956. The missile was a relatively big weapon and the programme involved many flights with various combinations of the missiles to determine the effect on the flight envelope.

Many flights were also made for jettisoning trials. The Firestreaks were carried on short rails and held in position by a shear bolt. At launch the missile was unstable and if the firing malfunctioned the missile tumbled, and trials were necessary to determine the path of the missile under such circumstances. Also, if the Javelin flew too slowly at launch, the missile was similarly unstable.

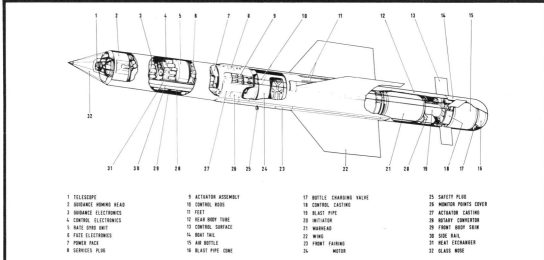

1 TELESCOPE	9 ACTUATOR ASSEMBLY	17 BOTTLE CHARGING VALVE	25 SAFETY PLUG
2 GUIDANCE HOMING HEAD	10 CONTROL RODS	18 CONTROL CASTING	26 MONITOR POINTS COVER
3 GUIDANCE ELECTRONICS	11 FEET	19 BLAST PIPE	27 ACTUATOR CASTING
4 CONTROL ELECTRONICS	12 REAR BODY TUBE	20 INITIATOR	28 ROTARY CONVERTOR
5 RATE GYRO UNIT	13 CONTROL SURFACE	21 WARHEAD	29 FRONT BODY SKIN
6 FUZE ELECTRONICS	14 BOAT TAIL	22 WING	30 SIDE RAIL
7 POWER PACK	15 AIR BOTTLE	23 FRONT FAIRING	31 HEAT EXCHANGER
8 SERVICES PLUG	16 BLAST PIPE CONE	24 MOTOR	32 GLASS NOSE

installation prototypes, specially equipped for the Firestreak introduction to Service Trials. The aircraft carried four missiles in addition to the standard armament of four 30mm cannon.

A navigator engaged in the trials described the Test Squadron's activities as follows:

'The normal sortie profile was to operate over Cardigan Bay when firing against Meteor U15/16s and Jindiviks — heights varied from sea level to 40,000ft. Speeds depended upon the firing profile adopted. The distance from the target also varied from long to short range, and some of our firings were at a much closer range than those which were eventually authorised for the operational Javelin squadrons. There were no firing controls in the back seat; one simply acquired and locked on using the AI, and gave minor corrections to the pilot when tracking, as well as range and countdown to fire. This last information was broadcast, and to help the navigator, a transmit button was placed on the floor — just had to keep one foot on it! This item became standard fit with the squadrons.

'The missiles were fitted with proximity fuses and the drones, Meteor or Jindivik, were often knocked down by a direct hit, but there was no built-in miss distance, and the missile was just as effective either hitting or "missing". Average sorties length was about an hour. The majority of sortie was just flying the missiles around — inert missiles that is.

'We also did some early jamming sorties with Valiants, on our part we had to devise a tactic/technique to intercept and to fire (using missiles) at a jamming target. All our reports went to the CFE where they were analysed.'

The Firestreak was powered by a solid rocket with a burn time of three seconds. This gave it a maximum range of four miles, and in close proximity attacks could be launched less than a mile from a target, although, with its infra-red guidance system, the launching range was ultimately determined by weather conditions. The missile could climb more than 10,000ft to intercept an aircraft flying above the attacking Javelin. The warhead weighed 50lb and could be either of the proximity or contact type.

Initial service trials were carried out by No 1 Guided Weapons Test Squadron, formerly the Guided Weapons Development Squadron, at RAF Valley. The Test Squadron had six crews and received the first of six Javelins F(AW) Mk 7s, XH901, on 13 January 1959. These early Javelins were virtually missile

During the course of these trials, from January 1959 to May 1962, 99 Firestreaks were fired.

The first production Javelin variant to be armed with Firestreaks was the F(AW) Mk 7, followed by the Mks 8 and 9. When missiles were carried the cannon armament was normally reduced to the two outer guns. Not all Javelin 7s were equipped with missiles as their primary armament; of the 142 built, about 100 were armed with four cannon.

The first squadron to receive the F(AW) Mk 7 Javelin was No 33 at RAF Leeming, and these were the four-gun version. The first squadron to receive the 'Firestreak' Javelins was No 23 at RAF Horsham-St Faith.

However, operational missiles were not then available and the squadron was issued initially with only a limited number of 'dummy' and 'training' rounds. Dummy rounds were painted black and were nothing more than suitably weighted wooden models used for display purposes and to enable pilots to become accustomed to the aircraft handling characteristics when loaded with two or four missiles. They were also used to balance a training round if only one of the latter was carried.

A training round, painted white like the real

weapon, was a much more sophisticated piece of equipment and was eventually standard issue to all Firestreak squadrons, both Javelin and Lightning, to a scale of at least one per aircraft. It comprised an operational missile case and infra red heat seeking eye in the glass nose, together with all the necessary electronics to run the eye and slave its conical search pattern to the aircraft's AI radar scanner over a small but very valuable 5° of movement. The rest of the missile contained dummy fuse sections, flight control gyros, power unit, warhead and rocket motor all correctly weighted and balanced to make up a realistic load. With the training round came an operational 'shoe', the attaching link between the missile and the aircraft underwing pylon. The shoe was made up of the missile launch rails, attachment lugs and necessary connectors to the various aircraft services and at the rear, the pressurised ammonia bottle. This ammonia played a vital role since it was the medium used to cool the infra-red eye of the missile and maintain it at the correct degree of heat sensitivity. It also had a significant impact on interception technique because the bottle only contained 15min supply. Since an

Far left, top: Javelin F(AW) Mk 8, XJ125, development and engine test bed aircraft, flying with four Firestreaks.

Far left, bottom: Firestreak armed Javelin F(AW) Mk 9, XH880, with the distinctive tail marking JHW, the initials of Wg Cdr J. H. Walton, CO of No 25 Squadron. The port of the inboard Aden cannon is evident; the outer cannon were removed on this version.

Above: A fine view of XH712.

Left: The first Javelin F(AW) Mk 8, XH966, climbs at height carrying four Firestreaks.

49

operational missile required 2min to arm itself prior to launch (run up flight control gyros and link the guidance system to the infra-red eye as well as get the eye itself to the right operating temperature) there was a limit on the number of times missiles could be 'armed' and held ready for launch during each sortie. Target acquisition by the missile had to be achieved therefore after missile arming but before expiry of the ammonia supply. Judicious use of available missile 'armed time' was thus another factor to be carefully considered by aircrew if more than one successful interception was to be achieved per sortie.

Training in this use of 'armed time' was, of course, only one purpose of the training round. Its primary role was to give aircrews initial experience and then regular training in achieving the all important 'missile acquisition' over the whole range of target heights and speeds without wearing out expensive and sensitive 'live' rounds.

To support the 'sensitive' live rounds when these become available, special Guided Weapon Servicing Complexes were built at the Javelin bases. These com-plexes were more like research laboratories than a fighter service bay, with technicians wearing white overalls in the clinically clean environment.

As experience was gained, the excessive zest for cleanliness was relaxed and the Firestreak came to be treated like any other sophisticated piece of advanced avionic equipment.

As is explained in the chapters describing the Javelin's activities in service, no Firestreak was ever fired in anger from the aircraft. Many armed missiles were carried on operations against potentially hostile targets, both in Europe and, particularly, in the Far East during the period of the Confrontation against Indonesia. In each of these theatres the deterrent effect of the missile was sufficient to serve its purpose.

The Firestreak was a first class weapon, highly thought of by its Javelin crews. It had a very good record and it exceeded its anticipated life by a handsome margin. Although production of the missile ceased in the 1960s, it was still listed in the RAF inventory in 1983.

Above right: RAF armourer mounting a Firestreak on the outer pylon of a Javelin. The glass panels enclosing the telescope are plainly evident.

Right: Firestreak and Javelin. Peace preservers.

50

6
With the Royal Air Force

The entry of the Javelin into service with the RAF in 1956 strengthened significantly Britain's air defences and helped to end a period of 'phony' air exercises. The performance of even the later marks of Meteor and Venom was quite inadequate for combating the new generation of bombers coming into service in Russia, the characteristics of which were represented in Britain by the high flying Canberra and the Valiant, first of the V-bombers.

It was not public knowledge at the time that, in order to give the aging Meteors and Venoms a chance during exercises, the 'enemy' bombers were often ordered to fly much lower than they would have done operationally. Without this instruction, the fighter pilots often successfully located the bombers, but could not complete the interception as they cruised some 5,000ft above the fighter's operational ceiling. Against such targets, they were allowed to claim a kill if the fighter was able to roll out of the final turn of the interception close in azimuth to the target, even though it was below and steadily falling behind.

With the Javelin no such concessions were necessary. The F(AW) Mk 1 had a maximum speed of 540kts at 40,000ft against the Meteor NF12's 504kts at 10,000ft, and its service ceiling of 52,500ft bettered that of the Meteor by 12,500ft. Its rate of climb was such that it could reach 45,000ft in under 10min, whereas the Meteor needed 12min to reach 30,000ft.

The fact that fighter pilots now had a 'tool' that enabled them to do their 'job', was undoubtedly a major reason why the Javelin quickly gained the affec-

tion of most of its crews, in spite of the continued restrictions on aerobatics and the early unserviceability teething troubles.

An indication of the effectiveness of the Javelin is given by the Log Book records of Charles Neale, an RAF Fighter Controller at that time. During the four month period May to August 1957, the log records 40 Javelin interceptions, mostly at night, all of which were rated as successful, while a number of those with night fighter Venoms were not.

The interceptions were generally Javelin to Javelin, and the altitudes for the missions rather modest, averaging 38,400ft. On the last two Javelin missions logged, however, the altitude reached was 45,000ft. The first of these particular 'high altitude' interceptions is interesting as it was 'for real', and was made to intercept an unidentified, and therefore presumed hostile, target coming toward the United Kingdom over the North Sea. The 'hostiles' turned out to be four Canberras.

Charles Neale recalls that, to him as a fighter controller, the Javelin 'gave the impression of having the flying characteristics reminiscent of a brick. It was fast and could reach high altitude quickly compared with the Venom, but its turning circle at altitude was an order of magnitude greater than the Venom it

Below: Javelin F(AW) Mk 4 of No 23 Squadron being serviced at Horsham St Faith during Exercise 'Vigilant'.

replaced, or indeed that of the Javelin's illustrious contemporary the Hunter'. 'Javelins', he explains, 'called for a hasty revision of control skills and techniques.' Few pilots, of course, would agree with the brick analogy, even though it was well known that the early Javelins did not have sufficient thrust to counter the high induced drag from the delta wing in a turn. Above 40,000ft it was general practice to limit the bank angle to 30°.

However, the Javelin turned out to be easier to control, as its relative lack of manoeuvrability was compensated for by its greater overtake speed and its much better radar. The task of a controller was to position the aircraft, using the ground radar, sufficiently accurately so that the navigator would pick up, in a good position, the target on the airborne radar and thus take over the interception.

Thus, providing a controller set a Javelin up reasonably accurately in the early stages, an interception was usually assured. The precision required from a ground controller for the middle stage of an interception with a Venom, was already in the hands of the navigator in the case of the Javelin.

Javelin F(AW)1s also equipped No 87 squadron, based at RAF Bruggen in West Germany. This squadron, and No 46, accounted for all the F(AW)1s not engaged on the development flying programme.

No 46 Squadron, at RAF Odiham, which pioneered the introduction into service of the Javelin F(AW)

Mk 1s, was also the first to receive the F(AW) Mk 2. The squadron began to re-equip with this version, which was basically a Mk 4 fitted with the US-designed AI22 radar instead of the British AI17, in the summer of 1957.

In August the new Javelins took part in the first Gunnery Meet organised by Fighter Command at Leconfield. The Javelins, together with Hunters of No 34 Squadron, represented 11 Group and competed against teams from the other two fighter groups in the Command, with Venoms, Hunters and Meteors. The contest was deliberately designed to be difficult. Each team, of four aircraft, had to fly three ranging and tracking cine exercises with the target aircraft taking violent evasive action, followed by two air-to-air missions involving attacks at a banner target. Sadly for the Javelin team, in spite of intensive gunnery practice and training, they came bottom in the night fighter competition, scoring only 837 marks out of a possible 2,000, due partly, it is said, to the unreliability of the AI22 radar.

The squadron took part in many other exercises, sometimes re-deploying to overseas bases, until July 1959, when Odiham ceased to be a fighter station and the Squadron moved to Waterbeach near Cambridge. It remained there until it was disbanded in April 1961.

Javelin F(AW) Mk 2s also went to No 89 Squadron, based at RAF Stradishall, the re-equipping from its Venom NF3s commencing in the autumn of

1957. Eight of this version were mixed with eight F(AW) Mk 6 Javelins, delivery of which also began in the autumn of that year. This mix of the two versions caused operational problems. The F(AW) Mk 6 had a greater fuel capacity, and was thus a heavier aircraft, with a slower rate of climb. It was not practical to mix the two in a 'scramble', and so whenever possible, aircraft of the same mark were operated together.

In November 1958 the squadron was renumbered to 85 and in August 1959, it moved to RAF West Malling, Kent. It was at this station the squadron re-equipped with F(AW) Mk 8s early in 1960.

The second squadron to receive Javelins was, actually, No 141, temporarily based at Horsham St Faith, while runway improvements were being made at its normal base at RAF Coltishall, Norfolk. The unit had received its first aircraft, a Javelin F(AW) Mk 4, XA637, on 8 February 1957, several months before the Mk 2 version had entered service with No 46 squadron! The conversion process was considerably assisted by flight commanders transferred from No 46 Squadron, the first Javelin unit, and was completed by March of that year.

The major difference between the Mk 4 and the earlier Mk 1, was the embodiment of a fully-powered, all-moving tailplane, to reduce stick loads at high speeds and generally provide more positive control in pitch. Another improvement was the vortex generators on the wing, to extend the buffet boundary and improve turn performance at altitude by allowing the aircraft to be flown closer to the stall with safety.

Deliveries of F(AW) Mk 4s to No 23 Squadron, also at Horsham St Faith, began in April 1957. No 23, incidentally, was the first squadron to have the benefit of the Javelin Mobile Training Unit to assist with its conversion.

In May Nos 23 and 141 Squadrons, together with Nos 41 and 46, took part in Exercise 'Vigilant', the most demanding test of Britain's air defences up to that time. During this exercise a force of 450 aircraft, including a number of the 'new' Valiant and Vulcan four-jet V-bombers, were used in the attack role. Such a force posed a severe test for Fighter Command, whose task was to counter the attacks well beyond the coastline.

This exercise was the first in which Javelins were used in squadron strength, and their performance under simulated war conditions was studied closely, particularly by the AOC, 12 Group, Air Vice-Marshal H. P. Fraser CB, CBE, AFC, who participated in the activities. Although one squadron night turn-round was accomplished in a commendable 10min, serviceability was not as good as it should have been . Lack of ground test equipment for the AI radar was a major problem. Nevertheless, the Javelin squadrons did achieve a number of successful V-bomber interceptions, making them the envy of those still operating Meteors and Venoms. The exercise clearly

53

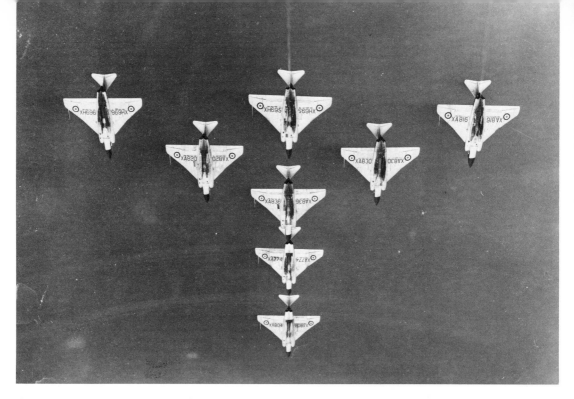

demonstrated the true potential of the Javelin as a versatile and heavily armed bomber destroyer, and indicated that the basic concept of the fighter was sound.

As is normal during such big exercises, most of the time was spent 'waiting around', but there was one three-minute action period recalled by Wg Cdr R. O. Campbell which provided a vintage Javelin story.

As dawn broke on 25 May two Hunters of No 74 Squadron (which with the Javelins of No 23 Squadron formed a wing operating out of Horsham St Faith) were scrambled to intercept incoming 'enemy' aircraft. As No 2 reached 36,000ft, its engine suddenly surged. The pilot shut the engine down, turned for his base and managed to relight the engine at a lower altitude. he arrived back at 'St Faiths' just as another Hunter abandoned its take-off and rolled off the runway into the grass overrun. Although no hurt or damage was suffered, the emergency service vehicles emerged from their huts and roared down the runway.

During these Hunter incidents, Javelin XA732 of No 141 Squadron was scrambled. It was fitted with the two large 'bosom' tanks and as it started to move the front attachment of one of them (an old bomb clip) failed, allowing the tank to swing down about its rear mounting. Because of the large delta wing, the tank failure was hidden from the sight of the crew. So the pilot taxied on, pushing the nose of the tank along the ground, the noise of this being overcome by that of the engines. The rough surface of the taxyway quickly

Above: An unusual formation flown by six Javelin F(AW) Mk 6s, and two F(AW) Mk 2s, XA774 and XA804, of No 85 Squadron.

wore a hole in the tank; there were sparks around and the leaking fuel caught fire, but did not explode.

To try and draw attention of the Javelin pilot, people started waving, jumping up and down, and ATC even fired a red Verey light. The pilot saw all this action, and wondered why so much fuss was being made because a Hunter had gently overrun the runway! He watched the antics, as he continued to taxi, trailing flame and smoke.

At last an ATC controller grabbed the local frequency microphone and shouted something like 'Aircraft taxying, you are on fire, stop your engine.

This shouted message was heard — by the pilot of the approaching Hunter with the sick engine — who immediately thought that *his* engine was on fire. He shut down the engine, and force landed across the airfield. The impact broke the fuselage behind the cockpit and simultaneously fired the primary charge of the ejection seat. Up went the pilot, still in his seat, away from the aircraft the remains of which continued to slide along the ground, demolishing two bicycles in the process.

Meanwhile, the Javelin pilot continued his taxying operation, quite enjoying the excitement of the second Hunter incident. The navigator at this stage complained that he was getting very hot. The pilot found the temperature control at 'full cool'. The navigator was just about to criticise the air conditioning system when he noticed an orange flickering reflected in his canopy. He realised something was amiss and shouted 'It's us — we're on fire'. Normal egress from a Javelin without the special ladder was over the trailing edge of the wing, but by now that was blazing merrily. The crew had to climb along the nose and drop off (14ft high). The only injury described in the subsequent report was to the pilot's feet, 'through landing in the running position'. Without exploding, the aircraft burned to a pile of ash, leaving a forlorn fin sticking skywards.

After the exercise, Nos 23 and 141 Squadrons returned to Coltishall, where they were responsible for the night defence of Eastern England. The availability of their potent Javelin 4s enabled the RAF to undertake more effectively the 'immediate readiness' role, which had been pioneered for two months in 1957 by No 46 Squadron. Code-named 'Fabulous', this had previously been the responsibility of the USAF. Under 'Fabulous', the aircraft were positioned on the 'scramble pans' (officially known as Operational Readiness Platforms) adjoining the duty runway, with the 'Battle Flight' crews, who were changed every hour, strapped in their seats and the telephone scramble-line connected. Two other Javelins stood nearby with their crews in readiness.

In September, Javelins of Nos 23 and 141 Squadrons, by then operating from RAF Tangmere, made the biggest contribution to a spectacular flypast of 27 Javelins at the Farnborough Air Display. In the 1958 Display, No 23 also contributed to an even bigger 45-Javelin flypast which thrilled the spectators.

In October of that year, No 23 Squadron took part in more war-like operations when it deployed to Cyprus to take part in Exercise 'Dragon'. Among the ground crews accompanying the aircraft was Sgt Mike Stiles, who recalls that at Nicosia the characteristic cloud of smoke emitted from one particular aircraft during engine starting seemed more volcanic than ever; so much so that it resulted in 'the fire service dashing out at each start'.

No 141 Squadron operated its Javelins for less than a year, for on 16 January 1958 it was renumbered No 41 Squadron when the squadron bearing that number at Biggin Hill was disbanded.

The fifth home-based squadron to receive Javelins was No 72, based at RAF Church Fenton, and was

the last of the Meteor NF squadrons to convert. Re-equipping this squadron began in April 1959, the Javelin F(AW) Mk 4s concerned having previously been in service with No 23 Squadron. Having soldiered on with the Meteor for so long, it was galling for the crews to have to accept No 23 Squadron's rather tired aircraft, especially as the three preceding Meteor squadrons (25, 33 and 64) all received shiny new Mk 7s.

To commemorate the conversion a flypast was organised at Church Fenton on 10 June. The highlight of this was a formation of three aircraft, a Javelin 4, XA755/'H', piloted by the CO, Wg Cdr V. G. Jones, a Meteor NF14, WS724/'P', flown by Sqn Ldr Hawkins, and a Gladiator K8032, flown by Geoff Worrall, Gloster Chief Production test pilot. The Gladiator was the sole remaining airworthy example of its type and flew at 184mph.

The squadron moved to RAF Leconfield, Yorkshire, in the summer of 1959, when Church Fenton ceased operations as a fighter base. No 72 Squadron operated its Javelins throughout 1960, the weekly routines of patrols, training and exercises, giving the aircraft a distinctly worn look by the end of the year. In February 1961, the unit transferred to Leeming,

Right: Nine Javelins, led by four Lightnings, taking part in the Queen's Birthday Flypast, 1962.

Right: A Javelin retracts its landing gear after a 'scramble' take-off.

Below: A fine silhouette of Javelins.

while the runway at Leconfield was strengthened, and was disbanded in June 1961.

The operational range of the early Javelin variants was rather less than was desirable, particularly when flying without external fuel tanks. This feature was improved on the Javelin F(AW) Mk 5s, which carried an additional 125gal of fuel in each wing.

The first squadron to be wholly equipped with the new 'longer range' Javelins was No 151 at RAF Leuchars, Fife, in Scotland where two aircraft were handed over in May 1957. The remaining 14 aircraft were, however, delivered to Turnhouse Airport, Edinburgh, pending the completion of runway repairs at Leuchars. By the end of the year the squadron was fully operational at Leuchers.

In addition to its normal routine duties, the unit achieved a reputation for appearing at air shows, where a four-aircraft formation displayed the combined excellence of both machine and crews. In September 1961 the unit was disbanded, some of its aircraft being issued to other squadrons.

First deliveries of the Javelin F(AW) Mk 6 were, as already recorded, made to No 89 Squadron, which received six aircraft in the autumn of 1957. This mark bore the same relationship with the Mk 5, as the Mk 2 did to the Mk 4. It carried the US-built AI22 radar instead of the British AI17. The second squadron to receive this variant was No 29 at RAF Acklington, Northumberland. This squadron was the first RAF unit to operate jet night fighters, these being Meteor NF11s when it was based at Tangmere.

An unusual incident in June caused the squadron to move away from Acklington. The wheels of one parked Javelin, the heaviest aircraft based at the airfield, sank through the concrete hardstanding, which had weakened due to subsidence in an old coal mine beneath the area. The problem was overcome by transferring the unit to Leuchars.

During May 1960, the squadron took part in the Fighter Command Exercise 'Yeoman'. While operating over the North Sea, two of its Javelins, XA829 and XA835 collided at 40,000ft. One Javelin started to break up and the crew ejected immediately and were later safely retrieved by helicopter. The pilot of the second machine tried to get his aircraft down at the nearest suitable airfield, Middleton St George, near Darlington, but lost control over the coast and had to eject. In the middle of 1961, the squadron began to re-equip with Javelin F(AW) Mk 9s.

On 9 November 1956, the first of a 'second generation' of Javelins completed its maiden flight. This was the Javelin F(AW) Mk 7, powered by two Armstrong-Siddeley Sapphire Sa7 engines, each developing 11,000lb thrust, — an increase of 32% over the thrust of the Sa6s which powered the earlier marks of Javelin. The new mark also embodied major changes to the flying control system, including a fully powered rudder and auto-stabilisers monitoring both yaw and pitch axes.

The aircraft was also designed to have a main armament of four Firestreak infra-red guided missiles carried on pylons under the wings backed up by two 30mm Aden guns. However, due to delays in finalising the fairly complex missile installation, the initial batch of production Mk 7s (some two squadrons of aircraft) carried the same four Aden gun armament as earlier marks. Thus, almost by accident, was created the 'sports GT' version of the whole Javelin range for with its 'big Sapphire' engines but lacking the weight and drag of the missile installation and the weapons themselves, the 'four gun' Mk 7 was an impressive performer compared with the earlier Mk 4s and 5s, particularly in rate of climb, a height of 45,000ft being attained in 6.6min, and manoeuvrability at altitude. Indeed, in these latter aspects, it even outshone the later, but heavier, reheated missile-armed aircraft, the Mk 8s and Mk 9s.

The first squadron to re-equip with the new Javelin was No 33, temporarily detached to RAF Leeming, the home of the Javelin Mobile Training Unit (JMTU), while the runway at their normal base RAF Middleton St George was being repaired and extended. This was convenient for when the first Mk 7 arrived at Leeming on 4 July 1958, the updated JMTU was immediately on hand to assist the squadron in its conversion from their Meteor NF 12s and 14s. Moreover, the squadron was able to draw on the full resources of the major unit at Leeming, No 228 OCU (the night fighter operational conversion unit) for the training of their navigators in the use of AI17. The squadron's conversion was thus completed quickly and by mid-August the services of the JMTU were no longer required.

By 1 October 1958 the runway repairs at Middleton St George were complete and the squadron returned home in time to take part in that year's annual air defence exercise, code-named 'Sunbeam'. This was an ideal opportunity for the squadron and the staffs at Group and Command to evaluate the performance of the new 'GT' Javelin in squadron service against a realistic simulation of the growing Russian bomber threat posed by the Canberras and V-bombers of Bomber Command. No 33's crews were delighted with the showing of their new aircraft and were quickly confident of their ability to intercept even the highest and fastest flying of the Vulcans which itself outperformed any likely Russian threat of that period. However, even the most ardent squadron enthusiast had to admit that the need to close to 1,000yd behind the target for the 30mm Aden cannon to be effective meant a protracted interception particularly when, in extreme circumstances, overtake speed was low.

Moreover, carrying out such a manoeuvre against a friendly Vulcan with no defensive armament was very different from attempting the same exercise against a Russian bomber, all of which carried radar-laid rearward facing guns capable of opening up at 2,000yd.

The answer to this problem was, of course, the Firestreak guided weapon and for some time the All-Weather Development Squadron (AWDS) of the Central Flying Establishment at West Raynham had been doing trials with three Javelin Mk 7s equipped with these potent missiles. Their task had been to evolve new interception techniques and missile attack procedures to maximise the tremendous advance in kill potential that these weapons gave the Javelin. Their Trial Report was now ready for dissemination to each squadron scheduled to re-equip.

Meanwhile, one of the features of the Javelin force at this time was that they were often seen flying in quite large formations; this was not to be when the Lightnings replaced the Javelin. Much of this formation flying was for public display purposes and during 1959 No 33 Squadron was particularly proud of its 10-aircraft display team. This gave impressive demonstrations on 9 June 1959, during the annual inspection by the AOC No 13 Group, Air Vice-Marshal A. Earle, and during the 'At Home' on 19 September at Middleton for the Battle of Britain anniversary celebrations.

Although some Javelin squadrons were based overseas permanently, as described in the following

chapter, most 'home-based' squadrons were deployed abroad on what were known as 'fighter mobility exercises' or because of local crises. Most of the routine deployments were to Cyprus.

Thus, most of the Javelins of No 33 Squadron went to Cyprus on 16 February 1959, when for three weeks they not only provided the air defence of the island, but also made courtesy visits to Greece and Turkey. This was followed in April by a week's visit by 10 aircraft, with ground crew, to Germany. However, the most important foreign 'excursion' by the squadron, began on 30 September, when 13 Javelins took off for redeployment in the Mediterranean area as the duty all-weather defence squadron. In command was Wg Cdr N. Poole, a dynamic character and one of the very few navigators in command of a fighter squadron.

For this duty, the squadron was based at Akrotiri, but at the end of October eight of its Javelins made a series of courtesy visits and flying displays in Greece. For this activity, the aircraft were based for three days at the Royal Hellenic Air Force station at Larissa.

On 13 November the squadron returned to Britain, the CO's aircraft, XH835/'NP', bringing home a memento of the trip in the form of a portrait of Pericles, a famous Athenian patron of the arts who lived some 500 years BC. The code letters 'NP' were, of course, the initial letters of the wing commander.

In April 1960 the squadron again deployed to Cyprus for three weeks. On 1 October 1960 the squadron received its first F(AW) Mk 9 conversion aircraft.

Above left: A pair of F(AW) Mk 6 Javelins of No 85 Squadron.

Above: No 33 Squadron markings comprised a horizontal band of dark blue, light blue, red, light blue and dark blue stripes across the upper fin and rudder, as shown on the right hand Javelin. These colours commemorated the Squadron's connection with the Royal Flying Corps, when it operated BE2Cs in the defence of North East England. When the Squadron was renumbered No 5 in November 1962, the bands were incorporated in the new markings, as shown on the left.

Right: Gloster Gladiator, flown by Geoff Worrall, Gloster Chief Production Test Pilot, K8032, and a Meteor NF14, WS724, piloted by Sqn Ldr Hawkins, take part in a commemorative flypast at Church Fenton on 10 June 1959 to mark No 72 Squadron's conversion to Javelins, one of which, F(AW) Mk 4 XA755, flown by CO Wg Cdr V. G. Jones, completes this unusual trio of aircraft. The Gladiator speed was 184mph.

The second squadron to receive Javelin F(AW) Mk 7s, again the four-gun version, was No 64, based at RAF Duxford. The unit's first aircraft, XH752, which arrived on 28 August 1958, was actually secondhand, having previously seen service with the All Weather Development Squadron at West Raynham, as was their second aircraft, XH747, delivered on 17 September. In July, 1960, during a detachment to Cyprus, the squadron suffered its only Javelin 7 write-off. The aircraft concerned, XH789, experienced a hydraulic failure and crashed at Akrotiri.

In December, 1958, No 25 Squadron, based at Waterbeach, received the first of its Javelins F(AW) Mk 7s, XH905, to commence the replacement of the unit's force of Meteor 12s and 14s. Of interest is the fact that the aircraft of No 25 Squadron were the first real 'Firestreak' Mk 7s in that they had underwing pylons and all the systems required by the missile, but operational missiles were not initially available.

In June the following year the squadron proudly displayed its new Javelins at the 'Open House' USAF displays at Alconbury and Sculthorpe.

The last of the four squadrons to receive Javelin F(AW) Mk 7s, was No 23, normally based at RAF Coltishall, but at the time, April 1959, temporarily stationed at RAF Horsham St Faith. The Squadron returned to its home base in July, before re-equipment was complete. The Javelins were able to carry Firestreaks and the squadron was involved in the development of operational tactics to ensure the most effective use of the missiles. The squadron, which had previously operated with F(AW) Mk 4s and 5s, fully appreciated the increased effectiveness afforded by the heat-seeking weapon.

In common with other Javelin squadrons, No 23 operated as two 'Flights' each of six crews, one engaged on day flying and the other on night operations, the duties alternating between the two flights each week. In command of A Flight at this time was Sqn Ldr M. 'Dusty' Miller, who after leading the second phase of the Javelin Mobile Training Unit activities, and completing a tour of ministerial chairborne duties, had returned to operational flying.

Under the Fighter Command training syllabus each Javelin crew was required to fly a minimum of 20 hours a month, about half of which had to be at night. Most crews exceeded the minimum monthly figure, except when bad weather or a period of poor serviceability prevented it. At the time Fighter Command

Above left: Javelin F(AW) Mk 8, XH982, of No 41 Squadron.

Left: Javelin F(AW) Mk 9, XH896, of No 64 Squadron, in formation with a Canberra, a Meteor, two Hunters and a Spitfire. Note the Javelin is carrying one Firestreak only.

Right: Canberra T11, XA536, of the Leuchars–based 228 Operational Conversion Unit, in formation with a Javelin F(AW) Mk 7, XH912 (top) and a Javelin T3, XH397. Formed in October 1957 the primary task of the OCU was to train crews to fly the Javelin. The Unit was disbanded in September 1961.

had peace-time weather limits of a minimum of 800yd horizontal visibility and a cloud base of not less than 250ft for a Green/Master Green rating using QGH/GCA as a landing aid.

One of the squadron's crews, Flg Off H. Stark and his navigator Flg Off P. Baigent, suffered an unfortunate Javelin 'double'. On 11 February 1959 the crew had to eject from a Javelin 4 which caught fire at low altitude, and on 1 September 1959 had to repeat the performance from one of the squadron's new Mk 7s during a night exercise. On the latter occasion Stark and Baigent were struck by another Javelin while flying at 35,000ft. Both ejected safely, but sadly the crew of the second Javelin was killed.

No 23 Squadron operated its F(AW) Mk 7s for just over a year, when they were replaced by Javelin F(AW) Mk 9s by the middle of 1960.

On 9 May 1958 the prototype of the final production version of the Javelin, the Mk 8, made its first flight. The aircraft was a significant improvement in Javelin 'technology', being powered by two Sapphire Sa7R engines having a limited reheat capability. This increased the normal thrust of 11,000lb to 12,300lb. The reheat system took advantage of the fact that the output of the fuel pump was greater than that required for normal operation of the engine. The 'surplus' fuel was burnt in the jet pipe to produce the extra thrust. At low altitudes the pumps produced very little surplus fuel and as the reheat system had priority, its selection at low level could actually cause a *reduction* in thrust. The system was thus normally only used above 20,000ft where the extra thrust from engaging reheat just about compensated for the weight and drag of the missile installation and the weapons themselves. Thus, at these levels, overall performance was restored to something approaching that of the earlier 'GT' Javelin albeit at a significant cost in terms of increased fuel consumption. A height of 40,000ft could be reached in 4min. Incidentally there was a maximum time limit of 15min on continuous use of reheat.

Other changes embodied on this mark included an improved windscreen rain dispersal system, a liquid fuel engine starting system, and a Sperry autopilot which could be coupled to the US AI22 radar to provide an automatic interception capability. Aerodynamic improvements included drooped leading edges on the wings and dampers on both the yaw and pitch axes.

The first of four Javelin F(AW) Mk 8s was delivered to the Air Fighting Development Squadron of the Central Fighter Establishment on 26 October 1959, for the further evolution of interception tactics with the Firestreak air-to-air missiles.

Shortly afterwards, No 41 Squadron, at RAF Wattisham, became the first operational squadron to re-equip with the F(AW) Mk 8, with the delivery of

aircraft XH978 on 13 November. Some Javelin 'historians' have expressed surprise at the selection of No 41 Squadron for the Mk 8, as previously the squadron had flown only Mk 4s and 5s, with the British AI17 radar. The arrival of the Mk 8 meant that observers had to convert to the quite different US radar. Perhaps, when the '30-year rule' allows this, examination of contemporary official papers will reveal the reason for the seemingly illogical selection.

In the autumn of 1960, eight of the squadron's aircraft were detached to RAF Luqa, in order to participate in the island's annual air exercise, 'Malta ADEX 60'. The Javelins did well in the various phases of the actual exercise, but experienced the highest attrition rate suffered by visiting fighter units during similar exercises up to that time. It is reported that much of the unserviceability was due to the unreliability of the US radar.

A major event the following year was the practice formation flying in preparation for the Queen's Birthday flight over London on 10 June 1961. No 41 supplied eight of the 16 Javelins in the impressive flypast. The major event of 1962 was the squadron's participation in Exercise 'Fawn Echo', held in Norway in August. During this exercise, the Javelins flew alongside the F-86K Sabres of No 337 Squadron of the Royal Norwegian Air Force.

The Squadron was disbanded at the end of 1963, the event being marked by a flypast over St Omer, France, where the Squadron had set-up its first operational base during World War 1. Of interest is the fact that during 1963, the squadron at one time operated both the first Mk 8, XH966 and the last one, XJ165.

The second, and only other squadron to operate the Javelin F(AW) Mk 8, was No 85 at RAF West Malling, which received its first aircraft on 2 March 1960. West Malling, although strategically placed as far as the air defence of Britain was concerned, had the misfortune to lie under the path of a major civil air route. In order to ensure that the Javelins did not come near the large numbers of airliners using the route, they had to leave the airfield on very precise, fixed predetermined courses. These rigid rules imposed unacceptable restrictions on the operational use of the base, and Fighter Command withdrew from the station in September 1960 — after a large sum of money had been spent on extending its runway in preparation for the Lightnings which were to supersede the Javelin.

Another matter of irony, and a sad comment on Britain's habit of organising some things strangely, concerns the radar sets in No 85 Squadron's Javelin F(AW) Mk 8s. As indicated previously, these US AI22 sets were notorious for their unreliability, and No 85, having previously operated Mk 2s and 6s with

these, were fully aware of their shortcomings. When
they received their brand new Mk 8s, they looked
forward to at least having the latest and most up-to-
date sets, with many of the early problems cured or
minimised by the embodiment of modifications.
Unfortunately, their anticipatory pleasure was short
lived.

The unserviceability of the AI22 sets was so bad
that there were insufficient numbers available to fit
new sets to all the Mk 8s. To make up the shortage,
sets were removed from the squadron's old Mk 2 and
Mk 6 aircraft which had been 'retired' at 27 Maintenance Unit, and fitted to the new Mk 8s being prepared
for delivery to the same squadron!

The Mk 8 was the final production version of the
Javelin to see service with the RAF, but another
variant, the F(AW) Mk 9 was to serve with no less
than eight squadrons in greater numbers than earlier
marks. The Mk 9 was basically a Mk 7 airframe converted to take the Sapphire 7R with reheat, but
additional changes included slightly drooped leading
on the wings and the provision on some aircraft for in-
flight refuelling and the ability to carry four 230gal
underwing drop tanks.

The first squadron to receive the new 'converted'
Javelin F(AW) Mk 9 was No 25 at RAF Waterbeach,

Above: Javelin F(AW) Mk 9s of No 25 Squadron, led by the CO Wg Cdr J. H. Walton in his personalised aircraft XH880.

aircraft XH760 and 767 arriving on 4 December 1959, to begin the displacement of the unit's Mk 7s, the first of which had been delivered almost exactly one year previously.

In May 1960, the new Javelin was displayed to the public for the first time, when the squadron provided one at each of five bases, three USAF, at Alconbury, Bruntingthorpe and Chelveston, and at Lakenheath and Wethersfield. However, when the squadron opened its doors to the public during the Battle of Britain display in September, only one aircraft, XH768, was available, the remainder being abroad on their first deployment overseas to Cyprus.

In December 1961 the Squadron left Waterbeach and moved northwards to Leuchars in Scotland, some of the aircraft flying from Waterbeach and the remainder from Cyprus at the end of their deployment. In November 1962 the squadron was disbanded, and renumbered No 11 Squadron, and then transferred to RAF Geilenkirchen in Germany.

The second squadron to receive F(AW) Mk 9s was No 23 at RAF Coltishall, which received its first aircraft in December 1959 and completed its re-equipment by July 1960. This squadron was the first unit to operate with the in-flight refuelling capacity, and even before re-equipment was complete set about the task of refining the skills involved in this technique.

To gain experience the Javelin crews used to take-off in pairs and rendezvous with Valiant tankers of No 214 Squadron for practice wet and dry hook-ups over the North Sea.

A successful in-flight refuelling mission involved a high degree of piloting skill from both tanker and Javelin, as the approach had to be made at a very precise speed. If the Javelin closed at an overtaking speed of less than 3kts the jaws of the tanker coupling would not open, but at more than 7kts, the Hose Drum Unit (HDU) on the tanker aircraft could not reel in the slack quickly enough, causing the hose to whip violently, the action often being severe enough to fracture the weak link in the probe nozzle. This could be embarrassing as not only could the fighter then receive no fuel, but usually the fractured nozzle remained in the jaws of the drogue, thus preventing anyone else on that sortie from obtaining fuel. The problem was so severe that a 'standby' tanker was often provided.

An optimum refuelling operation involved the tanker flying at 230kts at a height between 30,000 and

35,000ft, and the Javelin starting its refuelling approach from 100ft behind and slightly below the drogue. The pilot first synchronised his speed with that of the tanker, and then he would slowly increase speed to achieve the all-important 5kt overtake speed. Using the natural trail angle of the refuelling pipe as a sighting line, and using his probe rather like a mounted knight holding his lance, the pilot aimed for the centre of the drogue basket.

About 15ft from the drogue, the Javelin would enter the drogue turbulence and a little more power was required to maintain closing speed. Once a satisfactory contact had been made, the Javelin pilot would maintain his slow overtake speed, until some 25ft of the tanker hose had been reeled in. The tanker operator would then open the refuelling valve and fuel would start to flow from the tanker to fighter under high pressure. Depending upon the amount to be transferred, the position might have to be held for 10min or more, the Javelin pilot slowly increasing power to maintain his position as the aircraft's flying altitude changed due to the increasing weight of fuel taken aboard.

When the required amount of fuel had been transferred, the tanker operator would close the fuel valves. Even now, the Javelin pilot could not relax, as the withdrawal needed to be a similarly gentle and con-

Above: Javelin F(AW) Mk 9, XH768, in use for ground instruction purposes, before being acquired by the museum at Southend in September 1971. The aircraft served with Nos 11, 25 and 29 Squadrons.

trolled manoeuvre. Too fast a withdrawal and the hose would flail violently — a hazardous situation with both aircraft still in close proximity.

As soon as sufficient crews had become proficient at in-flight refuelling, No 23 Squadron was ordered to conduct a reinforcement flight to Singapore to demonstrate that the technique gave Britain the ability to deploy the fighters long distance, quickly.

Code-named Exercise 'Dyke', the long flight required complex and precise planning, and its success was largely due to the detail planning of the CO of No 23 Squadron, Wg Cdr Graham A. Chapman, and the navigation planning of No 214 Tanker Squadron.

Six Javelin F(AW) Mk 9s were involved, these leaving as three pairs on different days. Because of the difficulties involved, and the lack of an effective homing device, it was an 'accompanied' flight. That is, the Javelins flew in sight of a tanker all the time and a standby tanker was available at each in-flight refuel because of the risk of a broken probe nozzle blocking a drogue basket. The most critical tanking leg was

Gan, in the Maldive Islands, to Changi, in Singapore. Five or even six 'top-ups' of fuel were required. This meant that to meet the combined requirements of an accompanied flight and standby tanker at each refuel point, the whole tanker force of six Valiants had to get airborne from Gan to get a single pair of Javelins through to Singapore. Not very cost effective. At the time there were press reports that some delays were due to stops being made to prevent the Javelin crews from becoming over-tired, but in fact it was the tanker crews who needed the rests!

This flight was the first of several such operations, most of them for training purposes, but some of them 'for real'. In June 1961 the Squadron again provided aircraft for Exercise 'Pounce', a second long range deployment when eight aircraft were in-flight refuelled to Karachi through Cyprus (Akrotiri) and Bahrain. The pace of this exercise much more closely resembled that of an operational deployment. Useful experience was gained, the force taking five days to reach Karachi but only four days on its return.

The experience was soon utilised, for hardly had the Javelins touched down at Coltishall than a 'for real' operational detachment was ordered back to Cyprus to reinforce Britain's Middle East Forces during the Irani/Kuwait crisis that had just erupted. Although on this occasion tanker support was not available necessitating the aircraft staging through France, Malta and Libya, the operation was notable because each aircraft carried four live Firestreak rounds — the first time fully operational missiles had been carried outside UK airspace.

A sharp lesson was learnt. Because at that time Nicosia had no proper storage facilities for Firestreak, the missiles were left on the aircraft which were dispersed in the open around the airfield. As usual the red protective plastic covers that fitted over the glass nose cones of the missiles, nicknamed 'Noddy Caps' by the groundcrew, were left in place until the aircraft were brought to readiness. This was normal practice for aircraft on 'Battle Flight' standby in the UK, but it was soon discovered that, after a few hours of soaking in the hot Mediterranean sun, sufficient heat would penetrate the 'Noddy Caps' to melt the bonding between the glass nose panels so that when the caps were removed some of the glass panels came away as well and the missiles rendered unserviceable. Repairs were hastily effected, but the incident provided food for thought on the handling of such weapons in sub-tropical and tropical climates. The detachment remained on standby in Cyprus for the whole of July 1961 until the threat to Kuwait had subsided. That the squadron was benefiting from all its experience in overseas deployments is illustrated by the fact that when ordered home on 1 August, despite adverse winds in the northern Mediterranean necessitating an extra landing at Pisa, all the Javelins completed the five stages from Nicosia to Coltishall in a single day.

These long overseas deployment flights required great physical endurance on the part of the crews, who were enclosed for many hours in the cockpits. To demonstrate just how long they could operate under such conditions, the CO Wg Cdr A. J. Owen and his navigator Sqn Ldr D. Palmer, made a noteworthy non-stop flight in XH899/'L' from Coltishall to Khormaksar, Aden, in 8hr 34min. In 1962 12 aircraft, also led by Wg Cdr Owen, flew to Singapore and back. In 1964 the squadron began to lose its Javelins, as these were replaced by Lightnings.

The third squadron to receive Javelin F(AW) Mk 9s, was No 64 at RAF Duxford, the first aircraft being delivered in June 1960. As was the case with No 23 Squadron, in-flight refuelling practice missions

Below: A fine view of Javelin F(AW) Mk 7, converted to a Javelin F(AW) Mk 9FR, showing to advantage its long, lance-like refuelling probe and bosom tanks.

began immediately. Most of these involved wet and dry hook-ups with Valiants of Bomber Command, but No 64 pioneered compatibility trials with Sea Vixens and Scimitars of the Royal Navy, which were fitted with 'buddy' flight refuelling packs under their wings for this purpose. Most of No 64 Squadron's significant activities occurred while the unit was on various attachments abroad and these are covered in the next chapter.

Two other squadrons were equipped with the Javelin F(AW) Mk 9, Nos 29 and 33. No 33 Squadron, at RAF Middleton St George, received its first aircraft in October 1960, and No 29, at RAF Leuchars, in the spring of 1961. After completion of the conversion course, No 33 settled in to the normal routine of fighter training with the emphasis on 'bad weather' landings. In August 1961 the squadron was detached to Cyprus, returning in September in time to participate in the Battle of Britain day celebrations. Later that year the squadron readied itself for a visit to Norway to take part in a NATO air defence exercise, but the event, which had been looked forward to keenly, was cancelled due to exceptionally bad weather.

The squadron was disbanded on 16 November 1962, and re-formed as No 5 Squadron the next day and sent to Geilenkirchen in Germany to strengthen the 2nd Tactical Air Force.

No 29 Squadron was the last unit in Fighter Command to be equipped with the Javelin, the F(AW) Mk 9s replacing the unit's F(AW) Mk 6s during the first half of 1961. As a reverse of the case of No 46 Squadron with its Mk 1s and 2s, and No 41 Squadron's Mk 4s and 8s, the navigators had the problem of learning how to operate the British AI17 radar, which differed significantly from the US AI22 radar on their earlier aircraft.

As was the custom during this period of peace, the squadron first presented its new Javelins to the general public at an air display, the one in question being the US Armed Forces Day celebrations at Prestwick in May. The new aircraft were displayed in greater numbers in September during the Battle of Britain anniversary celebrations.

The first new months of 1962 saw the squadron going abroad several times for the routine detachment and redeployment exercises, generally to Akrotiri, in Cyprus.

In 1963 the British military authorities considered that the Near East area was deficient in its all-weather defence capability, and decided to rectify this by transferring No 29 Squadron to that area permanently. Thus in February 1963, the squadron left Leuchars and flew to Nicosia to take up its new duties. The squadron's activities in the Near East and elsewhere are described in the following chapter.

The last UK-based operational unit with Javelins was No 23 Squadron, equipped with F(AW) Mk 9s, and by then based at RAF Leuchars. Through government policy, the number of fighter squadrons allocated to Fighter Command continued to be reduced and, because of this reduction, it was considered desirable to speed up the re-equipment of the remaining squadrons with Lightnings. These Mach 2, single-seat swept-wing fighters began to arrive in August, and the squadron's last Javelin, XH848, left Leuchars in mid-November, 1964.

With the departure of this Javelin, the reign of the Gloster delta-winged fighter as an integral part of the air defence of the United Kingdom came to an end. During the Javelins' period of service, which spanned $8\frac{1}{2}$ years, it had served with a total of 13 home-based

Below: Two Javelin F(AW) Mk 8s taking part in the disbandment flypast of No 25 Squadron on 28 February 1963.

squadrons. Now, after the lapse of nearly 20 years, one can perhaps begin to assess objectively the part the fighter played in this defence. It can be argued that, despite its shortcomings, during the period the Javelin served with Fighter Command, Britain enjoyed a greater security from the threat of air attack than the country had enjoyed since the end of World War 2.

Against the high level sub-sonic bomber threat of the period, the aircraft had more than adequate performance and once the Firestreak version became operational, the Royal Air Force had the most heavily armed and versatile interceptor in its history up to that date. It provided a delightfully stable instrument platform with good layout and a comfortable cockpit which took the hassle out of bad weather operations, a reasonably good wide scan radar (in AI17 form!) with two-crew operation which greatly eased the workload under conditions of heavy enemy jamming, and a multi-choice weapons system which certainly took the sting out of any Russian bomber's rear armament.

Although the Lightning which succeeded it was a superb pilot's aircraft and another great step forward in sheer performance, its armament was limited as was, certainly initially, its combat time in the air. Also its single-seat configuration and somewhat narrow scan AI tended to make it rather dependent on good ground control.

In terms of potency as an overall weapons system against the enemy of the time, the Firestreak Javelin force possessed a mastery at least comparable with that of the present Phantom AD force matched against Russia's current supersonic mixed high and low level threat.

Right: No 23 Squadron Christmas card, 1962.

Below: This sketch by former engine mechanic W. Heiron recalls the moment when the first Javelin for No 89 Squadron was towed into the Aircraft Servicing Flight hangar at RAF Stradishall in 1957.

7
Javelins Overseas

As indicated in the previous chapter, most of the home-based Javelin squadrons went abroad on short detachments, generally for training purposes, but sometimes to reinforce Britain's Middle East forces during local crises. However, some squadrons served abroad on extended detachments, or were stationed overseas permanently. The first of the latter was No 87 at RAF Bruggen in West Germany, the squadron's first Javelin, an F(AW) Mk 1, arriving in August 1957. It was in fact the fifth Javelin squadron to be formed, being preceded by Nos 23, 46, 141 and 151 in Britain.

Conversion from the squadron's Meteor NF11 night fighters was assisted by the Javelin Mobile Training Unit, which flew out from Leeming, two Valetta T4s fitted with AI17 radar. The importance of the re-equipping programme was marked by a special parade on 14 August. The parade was attended by many VIPs, including the C-in-C of the 2nd Tactical Air Force, and was addressed by both the squadron's CO, Wg Cdr L. W. G. Gill DSO, and the station commander, Grp Capt A. G. Dudgeon CBE, DFC. By the end of the summer the conversion was complete, all 14 of the F(AW)1s allocated to the unit being in service and the Meteors phased out.

With the squadron fully operational, it began taking part in the regular exercises which are part of the every day life of fighter squadrons. The exercises included regular visits to the armament practice range on the island of Sylt, off the North German coast. These visits resulted in two incidents, both of which were

Below: Javelin F(AW) Mk 9s of No 5 Squadron, which was based at RAF Geilenkirchen in West Germany. The German-based Javelin squadrons maintained a Battle Flight of two aircraft, with loaded guns and live Firestreaks, at immediate readiness, 24 hours a day, seven days a week.

Left: Javelin F(AW) Mk 9s of No 25 Squadron at Akrotiri, Cyprus. The squadron provided the Near East area with an all-weather defence capability. From Cyprus the Javelins were deployed to Aden, Gibraltar, Iran, Malta, North Africa and Singapore.

Below: A Javelin T3 (front aircraft) and a F(AW) Mk 9 of No 29 Squadron at Akrotiri.

potentially very serious. During one visit, a member of the ground crew was testing the fighter's 30mm cannon when several shells went over the target and hit a German fishing vessel which was passing by peacefully. To prevent a repetition the height of the butts was increased.

The second incident involved an airborne sortie. Taking part in an air-to-ground gunnery practice, a pilot attacked the target in a shallow dive and then pulled out in a gentle climb. As he did so he felt a peculiar 'bump'. Nothing abnormal appeared on the instruments and as all the parts of the aircraft visible to the pilot and his observer appeared normal, the aircraft returned to Bruggen.

However, during the postflight inspection on the ground a large hole was discovered in one of the ventral tanks. The tank was removed for closer examination, which revealed a 30mm shell inside, the entry of which had made a neat furrow in the skin. It was deduced that the shell was one which had been fired from the aircraft, hit the target and then ricocheted up to strike and enter the fuel tank. In other words, the pilot nearly shot himself down! Although not unique, this is a rare occurrence indeed.

With its F(AW) Mk 1 Javelins, sometimes supplemented by those of other marks, No 87 Squadron served in the 2nd Tactical Air Force as a front line fighter unit, until a drastic reduction in Britain's contribution to NATO resulted in the squadron being disbanded in January 1961.

The second Javelin unit to be formed overseas was No 96 Squadron, also based in Germany, at RAF Geilenkirchen. Javelin F(AW) Mk 4s began arriving to replace the unit's ageing Meteor NF11s in December 1958. Only a few aircraft had been delivered, however, when the squadron was renumbered No 3 on

21 January 1959, making No 96 the shortest lived Javelin squadron.

No 3 thus became the third Javelin squadron to serve in the 2nd Tactical Air Force. The squadron, in common with other RAF fighter units at that time, operated at a high state of readiness. The squadron maintained a 'Battle Flight', usually consisting of two aircraft, at immediate readiness to counter any Russian incursions into Allied air space. Sometimes, an 'unidentified' aircraft was picked up on radar screens and the Javelins were scrambled, but the 'hostile' usually turned out to be a civilian aircraft which had strayed from its flight plan or failed to establish radio contact with Air Traffic Control. 'Scrambles', however, were the exception rather than the rule, and the Javelins were usually engaged in regular day and night training flights. The squadron served as a Javelin unit for two years, when it was again disbanded and reformed, this time as a bomber unit with Canberras.

With the disbanding of Nos 3 and 87 Squadrons in January 1961, there remained only two other Javelin units in the British zone in Germany, No 5 Squadron at Laarbruch, with F(AW)5s and No 11 at Geilenkirchen with a mixture of F(AW)4s and 5s.

No 5 Squadron began to receive its Javelin F(AW) Mk 5s in the spring of 1960. In September 1961, the Berlin crisis resulted in the squadron strength being increased from its normal complement of 14 aircraft to 18 aircraft. Less than a year later, in November 1962, the squadron was disbanded, its Javelins being flown back to Britain for scrapping. However, the squadron did not die, because simultaneously No 33 Squadron,

Left: A formation of No 29 Squadron Javelin F(AW) Mk 9 over land and . . .

Below: . . . over the sea.

equipped with Javelin F(AW) Mk 9s, based at Middleton-St-George, was renumbered No 5 Squadron and transferred to RAF Geilenkirchen in Germany.

Most of the F(AW) Mk 4s with No 11 Squadron, based at RAF Geilenkirchen, were 'secondhand', having previously seen service with No 41 Squadron. The Mk 4s were phased out of service early in 1962, these being replaced by F(AW) Mk 5s, the first examples of which had arrived in the spring of 1961. The squadron operated with these aircraft for about a year and was then disbanded in December 1962. Its duties were continued by No 25 Squadron, equipped with Javelin F(AW) Mk 9s, which was renumbered No 11 Squadron on 1 December 1962 and flown from Leuchars to Geilenkirchen on 13 December.

The objective of this squadron renumbering was to provide more of the potent missile-armed Javelins in Germany. Ideally, all four squadrons would have operated F(AW) Mk 9s, but there were not enough of these available. Thus two squadrons were disbanded and their numbers 'handed on' to units already stationed overseas.

With both squadrons based at Geilenkirchen, they co-ordinated their duties. Each took its turn in providing the 'Battle Flight' of two aircraft, which were at immediate readiness 24 hours a day, every day of the year. With the inherent intentions and desires of Russia fresh in NATO's mind following the Berlin crisis, the squadrons' aircraft always flew with live Firestreaks and loaded guns, so that any Javelins in the air were ready for instant direction to any problem area.

The Javelin F(AW) Mk 9s served well for three years, their task eventually being undertaken by the supersonic Lightning F2s of Nos 19 and 92 Squadrons. No 5 Squadron was disbanded when No 92 Squadron arrived in November 1965, and

No 11 Squadron on 7 January 1966 after No 19 Squadron had settled in at RAF Gutersloh.

Two Javelin squadrons which enjoyed extended detachments overseas were No 29 and 64. As mentioned in the previous chapter, No 29 Squadron, normally based at RAF Leuchars, was transferred to the Near East in February 1963 to provide that area with an all-weather defence capability. The squadron quickly settled down at its new base near Nicosia, the civil airport, although it was soon to be transferred to the RAF airfield at Akrotiri, and during the following years deployed its Javelins to Aden, Gibraltar, Iran, Malta, North Africa and Singapore.

In September 1964 the squadron sent four Javelins to Malta, to take part in the flypast organised as part of the celebrations for the island's independence. The squadron also provided a four-aircraft display team to take part in the Iranian celebrations on that country's Armed Forces Day. This detachment' involved a journey to Shiraz in an area lacking in navigational aids, the longest leg of which, from Diyarkabir in Turkey to Tehran, a distance of over 600 miles highlighted the aircraft's lack of range.

This deficiency was overcome when most of the squadron's F(AW) Mk 9 Javelins were replaced by F(AW) Mk 9Rs, able to refuel in flight and modified to carry four 230gal tanks on the underwing pylons. The inflight refuel probes were not used operationally, only for ferrying. For a typical detachment the probes were bolted on before take-off and removed after landing.

Below: Javelin F(AW) Mk 9Rs of No 29 Squadron at Ndola, Zambia, during the early stages of the Rhodesian crisis following that country's unilateral Declaration of Independence.

Above: Javelin F(AW) Mk 9Rs of No 29 Squadron, during the Squadron's detachment to Zambia, with a Zambian Air Force de Havilland Beaver in the foreground.

Left: The humid conditions made maintenance operations more demanding during the detachment of Javelin F(AW) Mk 9Rs of No 29 Squadron to Zambia.

The probes were quite heavy and about five men were needed for the installation/removal processes.

The four underwing tanks were also somewhat of a mixed blessing. They did not extend the range by the amount that might be assumed. When refuelling in flight, as the tanks were nearing capacity, afterburning was sometimes required to enable the Javelin to maintain station with the tanker aircraft. On such occasions, the fuel consumption of the Javelin just about equalled the rate of refuelling! The reason for this four-tank anomaly was that as more and more fuel was taken on board, the aircraft finished up having to fly at too high an angle of attack to give an efficient lift/drag ratio. The solution eventually adopted was to use two tanks only whenever possible.

The most memorable detachment of the squadron came at the end of 1965, as a result of the unilateral Declaration of Independence by Mr Ian Smith, the Prime Minister of Rhodesia. For reasons still not fully explained Britain feared that the new nation might mount an attack on the big hydro-electric complex at the Kariba dam, which supplied power for Zambia's vital copper mining industry. To prevent such an attack, Britain offered a 'defensive force' to Zambia, which was accepted.

The major element in this force was a group of Javelin F(AW) Mk 9Rs, from No 29 Squadron. Initially, 10 aircraft were involved in the operation, and, fitted with four underwing tanks as well as the usual twin ventral 'bosom' tanks, these took off from Akrotiri on 1 December, to fly non-stop to Nairobi, Kenya. The long flight entailed passing over Egypt, the unauthorised excursion into Arab air space resulting in an angry anti-British outburst from President Nasser. From Nairobi, the Javelins staged to their destination the civil airport at Ndola, in the middle of the Zambian Copper Belt. In addition to the normal engineering crews, the squadron was accompanied by units of the RAF Regiment for ground defence.

Conditions at Ndola were far from ideal, to put it mildly. Pilots and ground crew were accommodated in makeshift wooden huts, the local college and odd buildings at a nearby show ground. A flight of four

Right: Javelin F(AW) Mk 7s, XH719 and XH837 of No 33 Squadron during a flypast over Athens harbour.

Below: Javelin F(AW) Mk 8, XJ115, gets airborne for the No 85 Squadron disbandment flypast on 28 February 1963; pilot Flt Lt J. Hutchinson; observer Flt Lt J. Cooke.

Far right, top: Javelin F(AW) Mk 9s of No 64 Squadron, with refuelling probes, prior to flying out to Tengah, Singapore, to reinforce No 60 Squadron during the Malaysian Confrontation crisis with Indonesia.

Far right, bottom: Refuelling probe. This could be fitted quickly, allowing the Javelin to be ready for long-range deployment duties in a matter of hours.

Javelins was stationed at Lusaka, some 200 miles south of Ndola. Conditions were no better here, the crews living in the agricultural show ground. The humid atmosphere did nothing to improve the Javelin's serviceability, and to minimise the maintenance task and the problem of spares supply, aircraft operations were restricted to a few training flights.

The Javelin activities, such as they were, were observed with some amusement by the 'rebels' in Salisbury, whose last thought or intention was to 'attack' anybody. Their one desire was to be left alone, a hope denied by a remarkable degree of solidarity not exhibited before by the other nations of the world.

The arrival of the Javelins at Ndola was assisted by the radar facilities provided by Air Traffic Control centre at Salisbury, Rhodesia. Also, every time the Javelins took off some sort of clearance had to be obtained from Salisbury ATC. Relations between the two 'sides' were very cordial, and the ATC staff invited No 29 Squadron over for a game of cricket, but the idea was banned by the British and Zambian governments. However, some members of the squadron ground crew accepted the invitation and deserted to Rhodesia.

After six months the decision was made to withdraw the Javelins from Ndola. This was due partly to the lowering morale of the squadron, partly to the obvious fact that Rhodesia was not going to attack Zambia, but last not not necessarily the least, because that country's government became unwilling, or more likely, unable to underwrite the cost of the Javelin unit. Thus, with the underwing tanks refitted, the squadron departed for Akrotiri at the end of July, the return flight being organised via Kenya and Aden to avoid

75

infringing Egyptian airspace. Squadron activities back at Akrotiri were more routine and the accommodation much more pleasant, than they were in Zambia.

The routine activities included flying aircraft back to Britain for the embodiment of modifications and major overhauls, and participation in the annual Malta air defence exercise.

Non-routine activities included the 'writing-off' of XH884 in a novel manner, while some of the squadron's basic Mk 9 Javelins were being prepared for store on Malta. The aircraft's landing gear inadvertently dropped into a pit normally used for servicing the under fuselage radomes of Shackletons. As attempts were made to lift the aircraft from the pit further damage was sustained, resulting in it being declared a write-off. Once so sentenced, the Javelin was pushed over the nearby cliffs into the sea — a custom initiated during World War 2. A more conventional fate befell XH776 which was dropped while it was being weighed. The accident damaged the Javelin beyond repair, whereupon it was used for fire practice.

No 29 Squadron's role as the RAFs all-weather defence force in the Middle East came to an end in April 1967 when the task was undertaken by Lightnings of No 56 Squadron. No 29 Squadron returned to England and was disbanded on 1 May.

The second Javelin squadron to serve an extended detachment overseas was No 64, normally based at RAF Binbrook. After a number of short detachments to the Middle East, the squadron's F(AW) Mk 9 Javelins were converted to the Mk 9R standard so that the four 230gal underwing tanks could be carried. With these 'long-range' Javelins the Squadron was selected as the rapid reinforcement force for the Middle and Far East.

The first 'long-range' detachment was made in 1963, when 12 of the squadron's Javelins were detached to India, to take part in that country's Exercise 'Shiksha'. This particular detachment was made under the terms of the Nassau Agreement, under which Britain and the US agreed to support India if that country was threatened by invasion, and the period was one of rising tension along her Northern frontier which had been crossed in several places by units of the Chinese Army. The Javelins left Binbrook on 27 October and arrived in India the following day having staged and been refuelled in flight by RAF Valiants. This was the first time RAF warplanes had entered India since she had gained independence, although No 23 Squadron had visited Pakistan in 1960.

During the exercise the Javelins initially played the part of attacking raiders, but later reverted to their more normal role of interceptors. For the exercise, which was intended to test India's defence systems, the Indian Air Force provided a substantial force of Canberra bombers, and Gnat and Hunter fighters. Other

Left: Javelin F(AW) Mk 9 of No 23 Squadron at Karachi International Airport, during Exercise 'Pounce', June 1961. Note the safari beds serving as cockpit sun shades.

76

Left: A beautiful shot of a Javelin F(AW) Mk 9 of No 60 Squadron banking over a tropical lighthouse off Singapore.

Centre left: The same Javelin over Clifford Pier along the main waterfront in Singapore. No 60 Squadron pioneered the novel operational techniques demanded by the low level patrols required over inhospitable terrain, often in bad weather, during the Malaysian Confrontation crisis with Indonesia.

Below: Javelin F(AW) Mk 9 of No 60 Squadron over Singapore City. The aircraft is being flown by the then Squadron Commander, Wg Cdr 'Jock' Frazer, whose initials appear on the fin as the aircraft identifying letters. This was a deliberate arrangement in keeping with the normal squadron practice of the personal allocation of aircraft to specific aircrews as far as was practical. Normally only one letter was used, 'JF' was an exception.

aircraft taking part included USAF F-100 Super Sabres, normally based in South Carolina and Canberras of the Royal Australian Air Force. At the end of the exercise the Air Ministry issued a statement which included the following reference to the part played by No 64 Squadron. 'There was plenty of trade day and night until the end. The rate of "kills" per sortie flown was very high.'

At the end of the exercise only seven Javelins returned to Binbrook. One aircraft, XH765 had been written off when landing at night while in the hands of a USAF captain on an exchange visit. The remaining four Javelins were ferried out to Singapore to strengthen No 60 Squadron, which was being built up to counter the aggressive actions of Indonesia towards Malaysia.

Back at Binbrook, No 64 Squadron took part in Exercise 'Twelth Night', operating from Leuchars for this purpose. However, the 'Confrontation', as it is generally known, with Indonesia worsened and it was decided to send one complete flight of eight aircraft to Singapore. By a combination of limited staging and long in-flight refuelled legs, the aircraft arrived at Tengah between 11 and 21 September 1964.

The flight remaining at Binbrook was gradually run down, its Javelin 9Rs being disposed to other units, No 29 Squadron in Cyprus receiving most of them. The Tengah flight was increased in strength and took over the squadron Number from 1 April 1965. No 64 Squadron, now based entirely in the Far East, had its Javelin F(AW) Mk 9Rs fitted with two 230gal underwing tanks and two Firestreaks. Thus equipped, the squadron assumed, for the duration of the Confrontation crisis, responsibility for the detachments at Labuan and Kuching in Borneo, hitherto borne by No 60 Squadron.

Based at RAF Tengah, Singapore, No 60 Squadron played the major role in the air operations against Indonesia. The squadron had traditionally been associated with the Far East since 1920 when it was established on the NW Frontier of India following its distinguished service in France during the Great War. The Javelin chapter in the squadron history started in July 1961 when it converted from its interim Meteor NF14s to Javelin F(AW) Mk 9s to become the first night/all-weather fighter squadron in the Far East Air Force. The first of its planned establishment of 16 aircraft was delivered by HQ Fighter Command (Ferry) from Waterbeach.

The original plan was to ferry the aircraft out in four 'flights' several weeks apart, the journey involving 20 flying hours over 10 countries and using 15 staging posts. The first batch of five reached Tengah safely on 13 July, but only four of the second batch of five aircraft on 8 August. The missing aircraft, XH791, crashed in what was then East Pakistan, now

Above: Wg Cdr 'Dusty' Miller, CO No 60 Squadron.

Above right: Javelin F(AW) Mk 9R, No 60 Squadron, at Kai Tak, Hong Kong, in June 1967, with the city lights of down-town Kowloon in the background.

Below right: Javelin F(AW) Mk 9Rs of No 60 Squadron at Kai Tak, June 1967 in company with the last airworthy Spitfire of the Royal Hong Kong Auxiliary Air Force.

Bangladesh, after suffering double engine failure due to the 'centre line closure' problem. Both the crew members ejected over the inhospitable terrain, but only the navigator survived.

During the third delivery flight of four aircraft one aircraft was seriously damaged at Tehran, the extensive repairs required delaying its arrival in Singapore until late November. Another Javelin got no further than Luqa, Malta, when a refuelling incident damaged it beyond repair.

The first Javelin CO was Wg Cdr 'Pete' Smith, who served until May 1963, when Wg Cdr 'Jock' Frazer arrived just in time to steer the squadron through the most active period of 'Confrontation', including the time when the unit expanded to become the biggest squadron in the RAF.

78

'Confrontation' was an unusual war, largely ignored by the world's press, radio and television, which concentrated on the other conflict in South-East Asia — in Vietnam. It was a difficult war of relatively small 'battles' fought along the border of mountains, swamps and jungle separating Indonesia and Eastern Malaysia (North Borneo). It was a war of stealth and infiltration by Indonesia, against which was deployed a large number of British, Australian and New Zealand personnel supporting the Malaysian Forces.

Although Malaysia, the Federation of Malaya, Singapore, Sarawak and Sabah was not formed in September 1962, No 60 Squadron had begun operating a night and all-weather air defence 'presence' from Butterworth in Northern Malaya as early as March of that year.

Indonesia did not begin to 'confront' the new federation until April 1963 when the first incursions were made into Eastern Malaysia across the border of Indonesian Borneo, and in September 'Confrontation' was declared officially.

To discharge its duties during the 'Confrontation' crisis the squadron undertook a new role which was to prove extremely demanding to both its Javelins and its aircrews. Instead of the short-range high-altitude interceptions for which the aircraft had been designed and for which the aircrews were primarily trained, the squadron now flew lengthy border patrols at low level. The patrols entailed flying over inhospitable terrain in often atrocious weather conditions. There were no navigational aids available, and the accuracy of a patrol often depended upon the crew's ability to distinguish local landmarks such as an individual group of rocks, a certain waterfall or even a particular tree.

The missions were often flown down to 50ft above the trees so that the crews could look through the dense jungle and also to ensure the aircraft were seen by any enemy ground forces engaged in infiltration operations. To extend the endurance of patrols, the crews regularly flew on one engine, with the other one usually idling, but sometimes shut down completely by the pilot, so reliable was the Javelin's relight capability.

The low cloud level often entailed the Javelin being flown along the 'tunnel' formed by the valley, and sides of the mountains and the tropical cloud base. Sometimes the end of the valley required a quick start-up of the stopped engine, for the rapid gain in height required. The good acceleration characteristic of the Sapphire was appreciated at such moments. The Hastings aircraft also engaged on anti-'Confrontation' duties were not up to this manoeuvre and in such circumstances had to effect a rapid U-turn to survive!

The low level operations in the humid conditions resulted in a problem with the Sapphire. The conditions imposed unexpected loads on the engines, which of course had been optimised for high altitude performance, resulting in compressor blade fatigue with possible dire consequences. The problem was resolved by restricting the use of the 82-93% engine rpm band. To pilots this was a genuine nuisance, as it ruled out the 88-90% band normally used in a fast low level cruise.

Another, more serious, problem was that of engine 'centre-line closure'. This was experienced during high level missions at full power when super-cooled water was ingested from the cold virtually perpetual thick, cumulo-nimbus clouds. The water caused the engine compressor casing to contract until contact was made with the compressor blades, with consequent disastrous effects, although it was rare for both engines to explode simultaneously. The rather Heath Robinson-like solution to this problem was to fit abrasive pads to the lining of the compressor casing so that, as the casing shrunk, the tips of the compressor blades were worn away smoothly as they came into contact.

For their 'Confrontation' patrols the Javelins flew with loaded guns and live Firestreaks, in order to be able to provide an instant response should any Indonesian aircraft attempt to cross the border. It was during one of these operational sorties that the squadron lost its first aircraft 'in action'. Javelin XH836 experienced total hydraulic failure as a result of which the pilot and navigator ejected. Both crew members landed unharmed in the jungle, but it took rescue teams five days to locate them.

Indonesia's aggressive actions included flying Russian-built Tupolev Tu-16 'Badger' bombers over Penang and to counter these operations it was decided in October 1963 to base a detachment of two Javelins at the Royal Australian Air Force airbase at Butterworth on the north-west coast. Two aircraft proved inadequate and on 10 December four more Javelins were detached to Butterworth. The four aircraft concerned were flown out from India, being among those of No 64 Squadron's Javelins which had taken part in Exercise 'Shikska'. They were the first F(AW) Mk 9Rs to join No 60 Squadron, and with the extra range provided by their two 230gal drop tanks, proved particularly useful in the difficult conditions over Borneo.

By January 1964 the detachment at Butterworth became 'permanent' and was designated C Flight. As such it became relatively independent from the A and B Flights at Tengah. The unit provided the air defence of Northern Malaya, in co-operation with the Australian Sabre day fighters also based at Butterworth.

Early in 1964 the Indonesian Government declared its intention to use aircraft to supply its guerrilla troops operating in Eastern Malaysia (North Borneo). In response, the whole of the area was declared an Air Defence Identification Zone (ADIZ) on 26 February 1964 and detachments of Hunters from No 20

Squadron and eight Javelins of No 60 Squadron were despatched from Tengah to Labuan and Kuching to enforce it. This meant that No 60 Squadron was now responsible for a 1,600-mile long front, with 'Battle Flight' readiness being maintained at four widely separated airfields, Butterworth, Tengah, Kuching and Labuan. Each Battle Flight required two fully armed Javelins on constant standby, at never less than 5min and often at 2min readiness, 24 hours a day, day in and day out. Such a task put a heavy demand on both aircraft and personnel.

To cope with these extending duties, No 60 Squadron's strength was further increased by four more F(AW) Mk 9Rs which had been in store at 27 MU, Shawbury. To misguide Indonesian Intelligence the aircraft were delivered with No 23 Squadron markings on the fins, to give the impression they were merely on a normal short term detachment from that unit. Arriving at Tengah on 30 January 1964, the aircraft were allotted to B Flight.

By the middle of May, the squadron, with 26 Javelins, including two T3s, had become the biggest fighter squadron in the RAF. Later the squadron reached a peak strength of 33 Javelins, operated by 42 aircrew.

For obvious reasons, particular attention was paid to the activities of the Russian-built Tu-16 'Badger' bombers operated by Indonesia. Concern had been felt for some time as to whether the bombers had been modified to carry the Russian 'Kennel' air-to-sea missile. It was necessary to have photographs of a 'Badger' to ascertain whether the technical modifications required had been embodied. To this end, a Javelin was kept on special standby during daylight hours, the navigator of which had on loan a Pentax camera.

In the event, on 21 September 1965 the Javelin, piloted by Flt Lt Colin Holman, was on 'ordinary' patrol, when a 'Badger' was picked up and intercepted at 10,000ft at an IAS of 420kts. By a stroke of luck, the navigator, Flt Lt Bene Baranowski, had taken the camera along with him.

Colin Holman, recalls the interception as follows: 'Seeing the rear turret guns tracking us I rolled "belly-up" towards him momentarily to flash my four Firestreaks. The rear guns were then rotated to the

Above right: 'Badger' Intercept. The remarkable photograph obtained during the Badger interception mission described in this chapter. Note the 'non-aggressive' position of the tail cannon. It was learned, later, that the Indonesian Chief of Air Staff was on board at the time.

Right: Flt Lt Colin Holman and his navigator, Flt Lt Bene Baranowski, in front of their Javelin after the successful 'Badger' interception made on 21 September 1965.

non-aggressive straight up position seen in the accompanying photograph and this enabled us to close right in to get the pictures we wanted. The Badger descended down to about 3,000ft flying over the sea to the south of Singapore Island known to have SAM defences, and it was deemed prudent to stay in very close formation underneath him to await an opportunity to break away. The pilot obligingly flew out over the sea to the south-east of Singapore and we returned to base.' Later, it transpired that the Indonesian Chief of Air Staff was flying in the 'Badger' at the time.

During low level operations, the psychological presence of the Javelin was sometimes more effective than the potential power of its armament, and the afterburners, normally not used below 20,000ft were put to a novel use. Often the afterburners were used to deter would be border infiltrators since, to the uninitiated, the 'bang' of the reheats lighting up sounded just like bombs landing nearby.

On one occasion the Javelins used their reheat to save a Gurkha patrol which had been ambushed. The patrol was surrounded by an estimated 60 men and its position was serious. However, a patrolling Javelin made a few low passes over the area, cutting in its afterburners at the moment of passing, and caused the Indonesians to withdraw.

The effectiveness of this technique was again convincingly demonstrated during the very last 'Confrontation' detachment on 18 February 1966. No

sooner had the four aircraft touched down at Kuching after their flight from Tengah when the Army Command received reports that 'bandits' were infiltrating just to the south of the twon, and the Air Force was asked if it would assist. After a hurried refuel one Javelin, XH777, flown by Colin Holman, was scrambled. Shortly after commencing their patrol, the navigator, Sqn Ldr Geoff Moores, was lucky enough to catch sight of a hurried movement across a small clearing in the dense jungle. The Javelin then spent the next 30min 'beating up' the spot where the movement had been seen, banging in the reheat each time the aircraft pulled out of its dummy attack. This not only effectively inhibited any further enemy movement, but when the Army arrived on the scene, they were able to take all the intruders prisoner without a single shot being fired.

In addition to the operational activities, time was found by both Nos 60 and 64 Squadrons to take part in aerobatic displays and formation flypasts. One such display, was an impressive combined Tengah Javelin Force 'Round the Island' flypast to mark the imminent departure of No 64 Squadron and, consequently, the last opportunity for a mass Javelin flypast.

Some friendly rivalry existed as to which unit should lead the formation. Naturally, No 60 wanted to, but since it was No 64 which was going, they felt they deserved pride of place. The novel compromise arrived at was that Dusty Miller, as CO of No 60 Squadron, would lead the formation, but do so in an aircraft of

No 64 Squadron, with their CO, Wg Cdr Basil De Iongh, as his navigator. Thus, the flypast consisted of an impeccable arrow-head formation of 10 Javelins of No 64 Squadron, the lead aircraft being flown by the CO of No 60 Squadron, followed by a 'diamond nine' of Javelins of No 60 Squadron.

The 'Confrontation' activities reached their peak in 1965 and it seemed that outright war was about to be declared. Fortunately this did not materialise — to the disappointment at the time of many of the Javelin crews involved. Indonesia reduced her aggressive actions and 'Confrontation' officially ceased on 11 August 1966.

Thus, by the time No 60 Squadron's 50th anniversary approached in April 1966, pressure had eased and the Battle Flights at the Borneo airfields stood down, and the total strength reduced to 22 aircraft, 12 at Tengah and 10 at Butterworth. However, operational duties still prevented the squadron concentrating all its aircraft for the birthday celebrations, as three aircraft were required to maintain the Battle Flight at Butterworth and the remaining seven aircraft could not fly down to Tengah until the day before. Thus no rehearsal was possible of the flypast with which the squadron planned to complement the usual parade. To overcome the lack of practice, it was planned that A Flight would fly a 'diamond nine' with which they were familiar, this being cleverly converted into a diamond 16 by getting the additional aircraft to formate to the rear, each pilot being instructed to 'follow' his adjacent

aircraft. No greater tribute can be paid to the skill employed in both planning the formation and in its execution than the accompanying photograph.

As can be imagined, the prospect of 16 Javelins in formation, for the final time it was believed, caused great interest among the ground staff, who had worked hard to get all the aircraft serviceable. Normally, protocol dictates that they would have been rigidly at attention on parade with their 'eyes front' as the aircraft passed over the saluting base. To enable them to share their pilots' skill, the non-standard 'Eyes up' was given at the appropriate moment.

With the disbandment of No 64 Squadron in June 1967, No 60 Squadron became the sole remaining Javelin squadron, but it was obvious that its days too were numbered. However, even after the end of the Indonesian 'Confrontation' the squadron was kept busy. In that month there was an outbreak of communist-inspired riots in Hong Kong, resulting in four of the squadron's aircraft being deployed at very short notice to Kai Tak, the colony's international airport.

This was the first time Javelins had been seen in the colony, and the mission, which necessitated a long journey via the Philippine Islands, would not have been possible had not the squadron taken over all of ex-64 Squadron's 'long-range' Mk 9R aircraft. The Javelins remained in Hong Kong for only nine days before being withdrawn, but three more similar visits to the colony were made, the last one early in 1968.

Left: Impeccable diamond 16 formation over Tengah flown by No 60 Squadron during the ceremonial parade held on 29 April 1966 to mark the Squadron's 50th anniversary. The formation was led by Sqn Ldr Don Cameron, with Flt Lt 'Baz' Whorwood as navigator.

Right: The departure of No 64 Squadron from Singapore was marked by an impressive combined Tengah Javelin Force 'Round the Island' flypast on 10 June 1967. This consisted of an arrow-head formation of 10 Javelins of No 64 Squadron, the lead aircraft being flown, unusually, by Wg Cdr 'Dusty' Miller of No 60 Squadron, followed by a diamond nine of No 60 Squadron Javelins.

By April 1968, the squadron strength was down to 10 Javelins, in preparation of their replacement by Lightnings. The final disbandment parade was held on 30 April. As the squadron was to be disbanded completely for the first time ever after 52 years, the CO, Dusty Miller, determined that it would be a memorable event.

As a tribute to the night flying ability of the Javelin, the flypast was, novelly, planned to coincide with the moments of sunset and thus required very careful timing. Just before the sunset, a diamond nine, led by Sqn Ldr Don Cameron, flew over the parade. After the traditional inspection on the ground, by which time it was completely dark, five of the Javelins landed. Shortly afterwards, the last four Javelins flew overhead in a box formation with all eight reheats blazing. It was rare for reheat to be used low down and the effect of the long flames streaming aft was startling. The four Javelins then returned in echelon, again in reheat, before landing. The glare from the exhausts caused the pilots to lose their night vision, and to help them see the aircraft in front, a bright light, borrowed from Canberra aircraft, was fitted to the tails of the Javelins.

By now all the parade floodlights were off and all nine Javelins taxyed in to line up facing the spectators, with a crescendo of noise and a glare of taxi lights,

until all was silenced by a simultaneous cut of all engines, leaving just a spotlight on the lowering of the ensign and the sound of the last post.

The age of the Javelin had ended.

It was, however, not quite the end of the Javelin. The very next morning a request was received from the Singapore Armed Forces, for six Javelins for trade training purposes. This request presented minor difficulties, as by then some of the Javelin oxygen bottles had already been adapted by the local swimming club for underwater activities. However, the aircraft did make their last journey to Seletar.

Even this was not quite the end of the Javelin activities. One F(AW) Mk 9, XH897, survived at Boscombe Down, and continued to serve that establishment for another eight years. It is now proudly exhibited at the Imperial War Museum, Duxford.

For operational purposes, however, this end had come with the disbandment parade of No 60 Squadron on 30 April 1968. The end of the Javelin's maker, Gloster Aircraft Company, had sadly ended just over four years earlier, as previously recorded.

As was the case with its home-based contemporaries, the 'overseas' Javelins had done their work well if not without difficulties. The duties were performed better than most people tend to remember.

Also like those in the home-based squadrons, no overseas Javelin ever fired its guns or released a missile in anger, although there were moments during the Confrontation activities when fingers must have been itching on the firing buttons. Javelins serving overseas, however, can claim a distinction not accorded to the aircraft which served in Britain; they did suffer some battle damage. On record are at least two occasions when individual Javelins were struck by single rifle bullets during low level operations over Malaysia.

The fact that no Javelin fired its weapons in anger is cause more for congratulation than commiseration. The fact is the Javelin achieved peacefully by its deterrent effect all that was demanded of it in a series of crises extending half way round the world over a period of 12 turbulent years. Judged by its service record, the Javelin was a success of which all concerned, its designers, makers, ground crews and aircrews, can be justly proud.

Left: End of an era. The ensign is lowered at RAF Tengah, Singapore, at the end of the impressive flypast at dusk on 30 April 1968, during the disbandment parade of No 60 Squadron.

8
Javelin Marks

Javelin F(AW) Mk 1

The first production Javelin 1, XA544, flew for the first time on 22 July 1954, piloted by Dicky Martin. Powered by two Armstrong Siddeley Sapphire Sa6 engines each developing 8,000lb static thrust, it had a maximum speed at sea level of 709mph, and could climb to 45,000ft in 9.8min. The take-off weight was 31,580lb.

The aircraft was armed with four 30mm cannon, used in conjunction with a British AI17 (Airborne Interception) radar installation. The radar had a range of about 18 miles and had a target lock-on capability at closer ranges. The flying controls included an electrically-operated variable incidence tailplane with conventional power-boosted elevators.

Forty Javelin 1s were built, of which 29 were delivered to the RAF, equipping No 46 Squadron at Odiham and, subsequently, No 87 Squadron at Wildenrath in Germany.

The remaining 11 aircraft were retained for use by Gloster for additional development trials and for use by various Ministry Establishments, as follows:

XA545: used to help develop the all-flying tail introduced on the Javelin 4.

Below: Javelin F(AW) Mk 1, XA549. One of the first production batch of 40 aircraft, this Javelin was used to evaluate various types of radio and navigational installations.

XA546: fitted with a Gee 3 installation; also used for spinning tests.

XA547: fitted with four underwing weapon pylons for initial trials of the de Havilland Firestreak missiles, then code-named 'Blue-Jay'. Also used for handling trials with ventral tanks by A&AEE, Boscombe Down.

XA548: used by Glosters for stalling and spinning trials. Fitted with an anti-spin parachute, tail bumper, drooped wing leading edge and slats.

XA550: used by Glosters for various tests at Moreton Valence.

Left: Javelin F(AW) Mk 1, XA552, showing to advantage the two 'bosom' under-fuselage fuel tanks. Note the partly extended airbrakes.

Below left: Aircraft XA552 being used in 1961 to flight test the 14,000lb thrust de Havilland Gyron Junior DGJ10 engines as part of the programme for the Bristol 188 supersonic research aircraft.

Below: Javelin F(AW) Mk 1, XA562, fitted with Avon Mk 210 engines for use as a flying test bed for that powerplant.

XA552: used to flight test the de Havilland 10,000lb thrust Gyron Junior DGJ10 engines for the Bristol 188 research aircraft programme. Delivered to Rolls-Royce, Filton, on 6 March 1963. Only 11 hours flown between March and May 1963, when the programme finally halted. In May the engines were removed and used as spares for the Bristol 188.

XA557: used by Armstrong Siddeley to flight test the Sapphire 100 series engine. Later used by Bristol Siddeley Engines, Filton, for strain gauge tests on the inlet guide vanes in an attempt to establish cause of cracking.

XA560: used to test the Sapphire Sa7 engines with reheat, each delivering 11,000lb static thrust. Thus powered, the aircraft first flew on 30 September 1955.

XA561: used for spinning trials at A&AEE. It was fitted with an anti-spin parachute and tail bumper bar.

XA562: used by RollsRoyce for flight trials of two Avon RA.24R engines.

XA563: used for handling trials at A&AEE.

Serial Record
XA544-XA572; XA618-XA628, built by Gloster Aircraft.

Javelin F(AW) Mk 2

The Javelin 2 was basically a Mk 1 equipped with the US designed AI22 (APQ-43) radar system instead of the British AI17. The scanner dish of the AI22 was smaller than that of the AI17, which enabled the nose of the aircraft to be shortened slightly. The actual radome, however, was bigger, and was hinged, allowing it to be opened for servicing; on the AI17 equipped aircraft the radome was removed for this purpose.

Another feature of the Javelin 2, apart from the first few aircraft, was the installation of the all-flying tail unit.

The prototype, XD158, flew for the first time on 31 October 1955, piloted by Dicky Martin, and the first production aircraft, XA768 on 25 April 1956. Deliveries to the RAF began on 27 June 1957, although prior to this three aircraft had been operated by the All Weather Development Wing of the Central Fighter Establishment (CFE) at RAF West Raynham.

A total of 30 production aircraft was built, by Glosters at Hucclecote. Of these 26 were issued to the RAF, to replace the Javelin 1s in No 46 Squadron and also to equip Nos 85 and 89 Squadrons.

The remaining four aircraft and the prototype were retained for development purposes, as follows:

XA769: used for radar, electrical system and generator development.

XA770: used for armament trials at A&AEE.

XA771: used for development work in connection with the installation of Firestreak missiles. During these trials the aircraft usually carried one Firestreak on a pylon beneath each wing.

XA778: modified as the prototype for the Javelin 7. For this purpose the aircraft was strengthened structurally, the air intakes enlarged, the jet pipes lengthened and a pair of Sapphire 7s of 11,000lb static thrust installed. Special instrumentation was installed in the nose. The aircraft was demonstrated at the September 1956 SBAC Show in this form.

After the engine trials, the aircraft was fitted with Sapphire 203/204 engines and then used at Boscombe Down as a chase 'plane. For this duty it was painted a brilliant fluorescent orange. It was also used for Pressure Error Correction (PEC) work. On aircraft the pitot and static pressure sources never accurately measure the air pressure which is used for instruments such as the airspeed indicator and altimeter. Each new type of aircraft and each new variant has to be carefully checked to determine exactly the amount the measurement differs from the true one, so that the necessary corrections can be made to the instrument readings. To determine the 'position error' the new aircraft or variant is flown alongside a specially calibrated aircraft. XA778 was used for these duties until the end of 1968.

Serial Record

XA768-XA781; XA799-XA814; XD158, built by Gloster Aircraft.

Below: Prototype Javelin F(AW) Mk 2, XD158. The Mk 2 was basically a Mk 1 fitted with US-designed radar.

Javelin T Mk 3

In spite of its size and advanced features, the first squadrons converted to the Javelin without the benefit of a dual-control trainer. To prepare for the conversion from its Meteor night fighters, No 46 Squadron, the first RAF squadron, sent its commanding officer and a flight commander to Boscombe Down to gain initial Javelin experience. These then returned to the Squadron's base at Odiham to convert the remaining pilots.

However, the need for a trainer was evident, and Glosters had in fact begun work on such a variant as early as 1950 to meet OR278 for a pilot conversion, instrument and gunnery training aircraft. Although this project did not proceed, the experience gained assisted the development of the Javelin-trainer. Designed to meet Specification T118D, this was based on the Javelin F(AW) Mk 4, the prototype being assembled from Gloster-built components by Air Service Training at Hamble. This aircraft, WT841, first flew on 26 August 1956, piloted by Jan Zurakowski.

Another aircraft, XK577 was used as a trials aircraft by A&AEE, Boscombe Down, and is thus sometimes referred to as a second prototype, although it was taken from the production assembly line.

The major change to the standard fighter Javelin was the insertion of a 44in long section in the front fuselage, not to make more room, but primarily to counteract the aft movement of the cg caused by the removal of the heavy, nose-mounted AI radar equipment. The rear seat was raised $9\frac{1}{2}$in above the level of

the front seat and moved forward to provide the instructor with a clear view forward over the top of the student pilot's head. A greatly enlarged canopy covered the new cockpit arrangement.

The standard armament of four wing-mounted 30mm cannon was retained for gunnery instruction, and to permit the instructor to assist aiming, a twin horizontal periscope sight was installed, this protruding from each side of the fuselage, to provide a ready identification feature for this particular variant. To increase the instruction time per flight, two 50gal fuel tanks were fitted in the new fuselage section. Another identification feature was the pitot on the right wing tip, as well as on the left, introduced on the 11th aircraft.

As might be expected, the Javelin 3 was heavier than its operational counterparts, and had an inferior performance. For example, it took 22min to climb to 45,000ft, compared with 9.8min for the Javelin 1 and 2. However, this did not prevent it being a very useful training aid, and one aircraft was sent to each squadron for continuation training and instrument ratings.

The first production Javelin T3, XH390, completed its maiden flight on 6 January 1958, piloted by Dickie

Below: WT841, prototype of the Javelin T Mk 3 dual-control trainer version of the Javelin fighter. The periscope, fitted to permit the instructor to assist aiming the cannon, can be seen below the cockpit canopy, above the engine intake.

Martin and was followed by 21 more of the variant. The first trainers were delivered to No 228 OCU at Leeming early in 1959. This unit was disbanded on 15 September 1961, when it was considered that a sufficient number of aircrew had been trained to satisfy the demands of the remaining squadrons until they were phased out of service.

This decision, however, was subsequently reversed due to the operational activities of the Javelins of Nos 60 and 64 Squadrons in defending Malaya during the 'Confrontation' with Indonesia, which clearly indicated the continuing need for two-seat fighters with an air identification capability.

Thus, No 228 OCU was reformed on 1 June 1965, this time based at Leuchars, where there was a Javelin 9 full flight simulator in addition to four Javelin 3s belonging to Flight Command's Instrument Rating Squadron.

Some Javelin 3s were used for other purposes, as follows:

WT841: the prototype used by Glosters for trial installations of equipment.

XK577; used as a trials aircraft by A&AEE.

Serial Record
XH390-XH397; XH432-XH438; XH443-XH447; XK577; XM336, built by Gloster Aircraft.

Javelin F(AW) Mk 4

The first Javelin 4, XA629, flew for the first time on 19 September 1955, piloted by Peter Varley. The major difference between this and earlier versions was the embodiment of an all-moving tailplane, with the elevators acting as anti-balance tabs, as had been envisaged in the initial stages of the project. Earlier versions, up to the 41st production aircraft, had an adjustable tailplane with conventional power-boosted elevators. This was acceptable at low speeds, but at high indicated airspeeds the stick forces became unacceptably high, hence the change.

The new tailplane had been tested earlier on XA545, the second production Javelin 1. To speed up the flying and acceptance trials, XA629 was brought forward in the production line position from No 41 to 11, hence its early maiden flight.

The Javelin 4 also introduced another significant improvement, vortex generators. These were developed to extend the buffet boundary so that maximum advantage could be taken of the higher thrust available from the new versions of the Sapphire under development for the Javelin, but they improved the performance generally so that it proved worthwhile to fit them to all earlier versions as well.

As part of the programme to extend the buffet boundary, Glosters had also experimented with the

Far left, bottom: Javelin F(AW) Mk 4. The major difference between this and earlier versions was the embodiment of an all-moving tailplane.

Left: Javelin F(AW) Mk 4, XA636, served in Nos 41, 87 and 141 Squadrons.

Below: Javelin F(AW) Mk 4, XA630, shows to advantage the all-flying tail, and the distinctive pen-nib fairing over the jet pipes.

installation of Kuchemann 'bumps', as described in the following chapter. These bumps were streamlined bodies positioned at the wing trailing edge in order to weaken shock waves and reduce their separation. The bumps were extensively flight tested on XA629, and were successful, but the vortex generators achieved similar results at reduced cost and less weight.

Fifty Javelin 4s were built, 18 by Gloster Aircraft at Hucclecote and 32 by Armstrong Whitworth at Coventry. The first deliveries were to the All Weather Development Squadron of the Central Fighter Establishment (CFE) at RAF West Raynham. The first fighter unit to receive the new version, early in 1957, was No 141 Squadron, normally based at RAF Coltishall, but at this time temporarily based at Horsham St Faith in Norfolk.

Other squadrons to fly the Javelin 4 were Nos 3, 11, 23, 41, 72, 87 and 96 and 141 replacing either Venoms, Meteors or earlier Javelin versions.

The majority of the production Javelin 4s were used only for their prime purpose, that is operations by RAF squadrons, but as with earlier versions, a number were retained for special tasks either before or after their service role.

XA629: used by Gloster to flight test Kuchemann 'bumps' to extend the buffet boundary.

XA631: used for engineering assessment, radio and operational reliability trials at A&AEE.

XA632: used for flight development trials of the Firestreak guided missile installation. Aircraft converted to carry four dummy missiles on pylons added under wing by Armstrong Whitworth. After the trials served with No 11 Squadron.

XA634: used for flight refuelling trials. Modified by Airwork Ltd to have a probe fitted to leading edge of left wing. Trials confirmed earlier reports on WT827 that wing-mounted probe not satisfactory.

XA644: used by Gloster in the Javelin 7 development programme, until it was destroyed when it collided with a Hunter on 24 August 1956 during a test flight from Moreton Valance.

XA720: used for handling assessment, A&AEE.

XA721: used for handling assessment, A&AEE.

XA723: used for cold weather trials at the RCAF winterisation test centre at Namao, Canada.

XA724: used for Firestreak aerodynamic flight trials, by Armstrong Whitworth.

XA725: used for Firestreak aerodynamic flight trials, by Armstrong Whitworth. Later used by A&AEE.

XA760: after serving with No 11 Squadron, used by A&AEE as a photographic chase aircraft.

Serial Record
XA629-XA640; XA644; XA763-XA767, built by Gloster Aircraft. XA720-XA737; XA749-XA762, built by Armstrong Whitworth.

Javelin F(AW) Mk 5

One of the features for which the Javelin had been criticised was its 'marginal' range when operating without external tanks. This had been a major reason for the lack of interest shown in the fighter when Glosters were trying to sell it to various European air forces.

This deficiency was largely overcome on the Javelin 5 which had a new wing containing an additional 250gal of fuel. Provision was also made for carrying four de Havilland Firestreak guided missiles on pylons under the wing. Apart from several minor changes in equipment the Javelin 5 was otherwise identical to the Javelin 4. Only keen spotters could distinguish the two versions. On the Javelin 5 the gun camera was in the wing between the cannon and the wing tip; on the Javelin 4 it was in the wing root.

The improved range and endurance of the Javelin 5 was the main reason why this Mark remained in service longer than the four previous versions. During its service life it was subject to an almost continuous programme of relatively minor but, collectively significant, modifications.

The first Javelin 5, XA641, was first flown on 26 July 1956, by Dicky Martin. It was followed by 63 aircraft, 19 of which were built by Gloster Aircraft and 44 by Armstrong Whitworth. First deliveries of the new aircraft were to No 151 Squadron at Leuchars in May 1957. Subsequently used by Nos 5, 11, 41, 72, 87 and 151 squadrons.

Several aircraft were used for development purposes, including:

XA641: used for handling and engineering trials at A&AEE.

XA649: used by the RAF Handling Squadron, Boscombe Down.

XA692: used by Institute of Aviation Medicine, RAE.

XA709: used for G90 camera tests at A&AEE.

XA711: used in the Sapphire 6 development programme by Armstrong Whitworth at Bitteswell, and for testing vortex generators. Also used at A&AEE for ammunition temperature tests, gas chamber icing tests and as a chase aircraft. It was also used for pitot error correction (PEC) work. Among its last tasks, were gravel-arrested landing experiments.

Serial Record
XA641-XA643; XA645-XA661, built by Gloster Aircraft. XA662-XA667; XA688-XA719; XH687-XH692, built by Armstrong Whitworth.

Top right: Javelin F(AW) Mk 5, embodied a new wing containing an additional 250gal of fuel.

Right: Javelin F(AW) Mk 5, XA711, was used in the Sapphire 6 development programme.

Javelin F(AW) Mk 6

The Javelin 6 was essentially a Mk 5 fitted with the US-built AI22 radar, instead of the British-made AI17, and consequently had the shortened radome associated with the American equipment.

The British radar was fitted to about three out of every four Javelins. The American radar was used for two main reasons. First, it enabled Britain's all-weather radar defences to be complementary to those of the US. Second, it ensured that any potential adversary was faced with the problem of jamming two quite different types of radar. At that time it was hoped that each system would be used by about half of the Javelin force, but only a relatively small quantity of the US equipment became available, so that a smaller proportion was fitted with this radar.

The first Javelin 6, XA815, made its first flight on 14 December 1956, with Dicky Martin as the pilot. Thirty-three Javelin 6s were built, the first of these entering service with No 89 Squadron in 1957. Nos 29 and 46 Squadrons also used this version.

Aircraft used for development and other purposes included:

XA821: used for target towing experiments by A&AEE, then placed in store. Subsequently issued to No 29 Squadron as a replacement aircraft. After completing its service life, the aircraft was placed on display at the entrance to No 25 MU, Hartlebury.

XA831: initially the personal aircraft of the CO of No 33 MU, this was used for a programme of rain erosion tests by the RAE, Farnborough. The programme was initiated to determine the extent to which rain damaged the dielectric material from which the nose radome was manufactured. For these duties, which took the Javelin to many parts of the world including Libya and Singapore, large areas of the aircraft were coated with orange fluorescent paint, giving it a marked non-RAF appearance. While still so painted it was also used for tests by the Institute of Aviation Medicine.

XA834: used for handling and fuel consumption tests by the A&AEE.

XA816: after completing service life, used by the RAF Fire School at Catterick.

XA830: after completing service life, used by the RAF Fire School at Catterick.

Serial Record
XA815-XA836; XH693-XH703, built by Gloster Aircraft.

Javelin F(AW) Mk 7

The first Javelin 7, XH704, completed its maiden flight on 9 November 1956, piloted by Dicky Martin. This version embodied significant changes compared with its predecessors.

It was powered by two Sapphire Sa7 engines, each developing 11,000lb static thrust, compared with the 8,000lb thrust of the engines fitted to the earlier versions. The extra power gave it a very good climb performance, a height of 45,000ft being attained in 6.6min. Changes associated with the new engines included an extended rear fuselage and angled jet pipe nozzles.

Major changes were also made to the flying control system, which was extensively modified to include pitch auto-stabilisation and fully-powered hydraulic operation of the rudder with a yaw stabiliser. An electro-hydraulic three-axis control autopilot with an automatic approach and altitude control was embodied. Vortex generators were fitted to the wings, together with ailerons having thickened trailing edges.

The Javelin 7 was also the first production variant to be armed with the de Havilland Firestreak infra-red homing air-to-air missiles. In fact, the Javelin was the first RAF fighter armed with air-to-air missiles to attain full squadron service. The aircraft also retained the four 30mm ADEN cannon fitted to earlier marks. Initially, only the two inner guns were to be fitted, but most Javelin 7s had four, due to delays associated with the missile installation and the need to introduce the type quickly into service.

The second Javelin 7, XH705, incorporated the production Firestreak system as a trial installation, but it was not until the 30th aircraft, XH753, which was brought forward from its planned position in the production sequence, that the installation was embodied on the assembly line. All the earlier aircraft of this version were equipped with the missiles retrospectively.

More Javelin 7s were built than any other variant, 85 by Gloster aircraft and 57 by Armstrong Whitworth at Coventry, making a total of 142. Of this total, however, 24 were initially retained for various trial and development purposes.

RAF deliveries, to No 33 Squadron, commenced in July 1958; the version also served with Nos 23, 25 and 64 Squadrons.

A total of 116 Javelin 7s were subsequently converted to Javelin F(AW) Mk 8 standard and redesignated Javelin 9.

Aircraft used for development tasks included:

XH704: used for performance trials at A&AEE, and for handling trials by Gloster.

XH705: used primarily to test the Firestreak produc-

Right: Javelin F(AW) Mk 7 was powered by two Sapphire Sa7 engines, each developing 11,000lb thrust, and was also the first production variant to be armed with the de Havilland Firestreak infra-red homing air-to-air missile.

tion missile installation at A&AEE. Later used as a photographic chase aircraft at A&AEE for ejector seat trials.

XH706: used for handling and autostabiliser trials at A&AEE.

XH707: used by Armstrong Siddeley for Sa7R engine evaluation with different forms of reheat, as a flying test bed for the Javelin 8 installation.

XH708: used for engineering trials by Gloster and A&AEE.

XH710: used for performance, operational reliability, radio installation trials at A&AEE. Also used as a pacer aircraft.

XH711: used for autopilot and instrument evaluation at the A&AEE. Also used for Firestreak tropical trials in Cyprus.

XH712: used for handling trials.

XH713: used for tropical trials, Bahrain.

XH714: used for operational reliability trials at A&AEE.

XH722: used by Gloster, A&AEE and for tropical trials in Libya.

XH746: fitted with Sapphire Sa7R engines with reheat, as trial installation for the Javelin 8. Tests by Bristol Siddeley Engines, Filton, included strain gauging, relighting, booster pump tests and reheat lightings. Later used at A&AEE for noise attenuation trials.

XH754: used by Gloster, for handling and autopilot trials at the A&AEE, and then by the Structural &

Engineering Flight at RAE, Farnborough, for a variety of purposes, the most notable of which was a rain dispersal system required for the windscreen of the TSR-2. A variety of air blowers, mounted just in front of the windscreen, were evaluated. Some high speed tests were conducted at RAF Changi, Singapore, to take advantage of the heavy tropical rain associated with South-East Asia. For these tests the upper part of the aircraft was painted a bright gloss white. During a visit to the RAAF base at Butterworth in Malaysia, the aircraft gained a red Kangaroo logo on the rear fuselage. This complemented a black Kiwi previously added by RNZAF personnel at Changi.

The aircraft then returned to Britain, where it was used in parachute trials at the weapons range at Larkhill. For these tests the aircraft had its nose and tail painted in dayglo orange, and black and white stripes added to its underside. The multi-coloured aircraft was affectionately referred to as the 'Javelin $7\frac{1}{2}$' by personnel at the RAE.

XH756: used for missile trials.

XH757: used by A&AEE for tropical trials, Kano, Nigeria.

XH759: used for handling trials at A&AEE.

XH780: fitted with refuelling probe by Flight Refuelling for flight trials of the installation.

XH783: used by the A&AEE, and the Guided Weapons Test squadron at Valley.

XH897: after service with No 5 Squadron, the aircraft was used by Bristol Siddeley Engines, Filton, to

investigate a compressor blade vibration problem which arose when Javelins began to be used extensively in the low level role.

The aircraft was then used by A&AEE as a PE calibration aircraft, and was used to calibrate the Aberporth range for supersonic PE measurements for the Concorde programme. Aircraft now in the Imperial War Museum, Duxford.

Serial Record
XH704-XH725; XH746-XH784; XH900-XH912; XH955-XH965, by Gloster Aircraft.
XH785-XH795; XH833-XH849; XH871-XH899, by Armstrong Whitworth.

Javelin F(AW) Mk 8
The first Javelin 8, XH966, flew for the first time on 9 May 1958, piloted by Dicky Martin.

This Mark was the final production version of the Javelin, and was powered by two Sapphire Sa7R engines each normally developing 11,000lb thrust. The engine had a limited reheat capability, operable above 20,000ft. Above this height the system provided a 12% increase in thrust, raising the total to 12,300lb.

This significantly improved the Javelin's already excellent rate of climb. A height of 40,000ft could be reached in 4min, this involving a $2\frac{1}{2}$min 'cold' climb to 20,000ft, then another $1\frac{1}{2}$min with reheat to 40,000ft.

Below: Javelin F(AW) Mk 8. This was the final production version of the Javelin, and was fitted with Sapphire Sa7R engines, with a limited reheat capacity. Aircraft XH966 was the first of a production batch of 47 aircraft.

The version could reach 50,000ft in just over 9min, a performance which surprised many of its critics as it was superior to that of the Hunter. The aircraft could also out-turn a Hunter and its armament was also greatly superior.

The reheat system took advantage of the fact that the output of the fuel pump was greater than that required for normal operation of the engine. It was this 'surplus' fuel that was injected into the jet pipe and burnt to augment the thrust. At low altitudes the main engine had very little surplus fuel and, as the reheat system had priority, selection of reheat at low level could actually cause the engine to slow down by a few per cent, thus actually losing thrust. However, the system produced a thunderous roar when selected under such conditions. As described in Chapter 7, the noise was used as an airborne 'frightener' during the troubles in Malaysia.

The reheat system gave the Javelin 8 its biggest external difference from earlier versions, each jet pipe being fitted with a nozzle embodying twenty-seven distinctive inter-leaved segments.

Equipment changes included the installation of a Sperry autopilot, a Gloster-developed pitch auto-stabiliser, a Louis Newmark yaw stabiliser, and a fully-powered rudder. The wing leading edge was drooped and the wing had two rows of vortex generators.

The standard armament was four Firestreak air-to-air missiles on underwing pylons and two 30mm Aden guns in the outer position in the wings. The associated radar was the US-built AI22. The Mark 8 was the first and only Javelin to use the Sperry autopilot. This could be coupled to the AI to provide a full 'lock-on'

capability. This meant that a complete interception sequence could be performed automatically, without either crew member actually seeing the target.

The aerodynamics of the Mk 8 were improved by the wing drooped leading edges. An unfortunate 'side-effect' of the new leading edge was that in association with the underwing missile pylons it altered the pattern of the airflow in the vicinity of the stall warning sensing vanes, so that the stall warning system became unreliable under certain conditions. At the time Gloster proposed that the vanes should be repositioned, and conducted trials in 1961, but no squadron aircraft were modified, the Ministry view being that the existing limitations on Javelin manoeuvres, if strictly observed, ensured that crews were not exposed to unacceptable danger.

The Javelin 8 also introduced a new, liquid-fuel, engine starting system. As described in Chapter 4, this utilised a relatively small cordite cartridge to ignite the liquid fuel, the resulting gas generating increased pressure which was fed to the starter turbine.

Another feature introduced on this mark was an improved windscreen rain dispersal system, in spite of the Javelin's already good visibility in rain or misty conditions. The new system directed a stream of hot air over the front windscreen, the hot air being cut-off by a barometric valve above 10,000ft to avoid the possibility of the windscreen cracking.

The first squadron to receive Javelin 8s was No 41 in the spring of 1960. Other squadrons which operated this version included Nos 23, 72 and 85.

Forty-seven Javelin 8s were built, all by Glosters at Hucclecote. The last one of the production batch, XJ165, left Moreton Valance on 16 August 1960, on a delivery flight to No 41 Squadron. This was the 435th Javelin and the last aircraft to be built by Glosters.

Aircraft used for special purposes included:

XH966: used for flying trials by Gloster. Exhibited at the 1958 SBAC Show at Farnborough. Used for high altitude and gun armament trials at the A&AEE.

XH967: used for radio and armament trials at the A&AEE.

XH968: used for radio and armament trials at the A&AEE and for development work by Gloster.

XH969: used for handling and autopilot trials by 'A' Squadron at the A&AEE.

XH970: used for handling assessment trials by Glosters, then for autopilot trials at the A&AEE. Also used for unusual jettison and braking trials, when fitted with 230gal underwing tanks, the tanks being jettisoned during taxying and take-off runs.

XJ112: not a 'genuine' Javelin, as it was never completed to flight standard but is included here as it was taken from the production line for static tests.

XJ125: the second Javelin 8 to be built, used by Armstrong Siddeley for development trials on the Sapphire Sa7R engine. The tests involved an extensive flying programme with the first flight being made at 8.00am and flying continuing until 11.00pm, every day, with only minimum periods on the ground for refuelling and changes of crew. Exhibited at the 1959 SBAC Show at Farnborough.

Serial Record
XH966-XH993; XJ113-XJ130; XJ165, built by Gloster Aircraft.

Javelin F(AW) Mk 9

In spite of its new designation, the Javelin 9 was not a new variant built on the production line. The version was basically an F(AW) Mk 7 airframe converted to take the Sapphire Sa7R with reheat.

Although the Javelin 7 had a good performance, it lacked at high altitude the manouevrability of its more powerful successor, the Javelin 8, with its reheated Sapphire and aerodynamic refinements.

Accordingly, in 1960 the decision was taken to modify a large number of Javelin 7s, to bring them up to the same standard as the Javelin 8. When so converted, they were redesignated Javelin F(AW) Mk 9.

The conversion process involved a major rebuild operating taking many hundreds of manhours. For conversion, each Javelin 7 was returned to Glosters, Moreton Valence, where the existing engines were removed and the airframe broken down into major components. In this state, each mainplane was modified to have the slightly drooped leading edge as fitted to the Javelin 8.

Changes associated with the new engines included the installation of the liquid fuel starting system, engine de-icing and an improved windscreen rain dispersal system.

System changes included a four-pump hydraulic system, an improved tailplane trimming system, a fully-powered rudder, and pitch and yaw dampers. New Martin Baker 3JS ejector seats were installed, together with a new oxygen regulator and provision for the crew to wear the ventilated suits developed by the Institute of Aviation Medicine.

The loss, in the early 1960s, of many RAF bases and staging airfields around the world, particularly in the Middle East and the Far East, drew attention to the need for extended ranges of all RAF aircraft, especially fighters. In-flight refuelling was the obvious answer. Thus, following the earlier, unsatisfactory, trial installations of wing-mounted probes, further tests were made with a huge, lance-like probe mounted on the right side of the fuselage nose. These trials, with Valiant and Canberra tankers, were much more satisfactory and 22 Javelin 9s were modified to accept the probe. The probe could be installed quickly, allowing the fighter to be made available for long-range deployment in a few hours. The potential of the system was dramatically demonstrated in October 1960, when four Javelin 9s of No 23 Squadron flew from Britain to Singapore, refuelling from Valiant tanker aircraft, with only three intermediate stops.

Most of the Javelins fitted for in-flight refuelling, were also modified to carry up to four 230gal under-wing drop tanks, after which they were designated Javelin F(AW) Mk 9R, the 'R' standing for range. The drop tanks were carried on the missile pylons, and to accommodate the tanks the inner pylons were canted outboard noticeably so that the tank cleared the main landing gear during retraction.

The first of the refurbished Javelin 7s entered service with No 25 Squadron in December 1959. Subsequently, deliveries were also made to Nos 23, 29, 33, 60 and 64 Squadrons.

A number of Javelin 9s were used for special purposes, including:

XH759: used by the A&AEE, and Glosters for radio and roll-damping trials.

XH780: used by Flight Refuelling for in-flight refuelling trials.

XH891: used by the A&AEE, for camera trials.

XH897: used at A&AEE for position error correction and photo chase duties. In 1968, painted a vivid red and white, it was used for pressure error pacing, photo-chase duties in connection with the Shorts special Canberra PR9, and calibration of Concorde 001 and MRCA test aircraft.

XH962: used for flight refuelling trials.

XH964: used by the A&AEE for radio trials.

XH965: used by Flight Refuelling for in-flight refuel-

ling trials. Also used by the A&AEE, and the RAE, Bedford, for ground trials.

Serial Record

In these lists, the Javelin F(AW) Mk 7 conversions to F(AW) Mks 9 and 9R are shown.

Conversion to Mk 9 (F/R) then to Mk 9R:
XH707-709, XH712, XH759, XH762-766, XH793, XH843, XH845, XH847, XH848, XH871-874, XH876, XH877, XH879, XH855-896, XH899, XH908, XH955, XH959, XH961, XH965.

Conversion to Mk 9 (F/R):
XH780, XH844, XH875, XH878

Conversion to Mk 9:
XH711, XH713, XH715, 716-719, XH721-725, XH747, XH749, XH751-753, XH755-758, XH760, XH761, XH761-774, XH776-779, XH785, 787, 788, XH791, XH792, XH794, XH833-836, XH839-842, XH846, XH880-XH884, XH897, XH898, XH903-907, XH909-912, XH956-958, XH960, XH962-964.

The designation Mk 9(F/R) indicates that the aircraft incorporated the necessary piping and valves required for in-flight refuelling. The designation Mk 9R indicates in-flight refuelling and provision to carry up to four 230gal 'long-range' auxiliary fuel tanks on the underwing missiles pylons.

Above right: Javelin F(AW) Mk 9 was the designation given to Mk 7 aircraft modified to Mk 8 standard.

Right: Javelin F(AW) Mk 9R. The suffix R denoted that, in addition to the refuelling probe, the aircraft could carry up to four 230gal under-wing drop tanks.

Left: Javelin F(AW) Mk 9, XH897 saw service as a Mk 7 with Nos 5, 25 and 33 Squadrons before being converted to a Mk 9. In this form it was delivered to Boscombe Down for Position Error Correction, photo chase duties, and calibration of Concorde and MRCA test aircraft. In this photograph XH897 is making its last public display at Coltishall on 30 September 1974. The final flight was made on 24 January 1975, when it flew from Boscombe Down, via the old Gloster works at Hucclecote, to Duxford, where it now forms part of the Imperial War Museum collection of historic aircraft. Total flying hours for XH897 was 1,690.

Below: Javelin F(AW) Mk 9, XH905, at No 27 MU shortly before the aircraft was scrapped.

9
Projects and Proposals

One of the factors which attracted the Ministry of Supply in its choice of the Javelin when it was in competition with the de Havilland DH110, was its potential for future development. Features indicating the potential included the relatively low wing loading, 32lb/sq ft, at a combat weight of 28,700lb, the large internal capacity available for additional fuel or military equipment, and the fact that more powerful engines of up to 12,000lb static thrust, could be installed with relatively minor airframe structural alterations. This claim was to be fully justified as, during its 11-year service life, the Javelin was to evolve through nine major variants. But for a fundamental change in Government policy it could have been several more.

In addition to these service variants, there were many interesting projects and proposals which were examined, some of which were flight tested, but which did not reach the production stage. One of the latter involved the installation of what are known as Kuchemann or Whitcombe 'bumps'. Known

irreverently as Gloster 'carrots', these were streamlined cone-shaped bodies fitted to the trailing edge of the wing, initially just inboard of the ailerons, but also later at the wing tips. The purpose of the 'carrots' was to weaken the shock waves around the wing and so reduce separation at high subsonic speeds to extend the buffet boundary.

Extensive wind tunnel tests indicated the value of such bodies and this was confirmed during some 30 hours of actual flight testing on aircraft XA629, the first Javelin 4. But excessive cost and weight precluded the adoption of the bodies in production. A similar benefit was obtained, at lower cost and weight, by adding two rows of vortex-generators along the leading edge of the outer wing panels and by thickening the trailing edges of the ailerons.

Kuchemann 'carrots' were also a feature of P316, a design study completed in May 1950 for a long-range fighter development of the Javelin. This was a single-seat aircraft, with a finely pointed nose as no radar

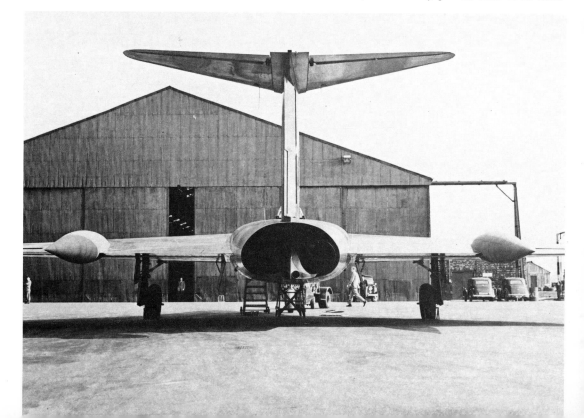

Below left: Kucheman streamlined bodies added to the wing trailing edge of aircraft XA629 to weaken shock waves and so extend the buffet boundary.

Right: Another view of one of the bodies, known irreverently as Gloster 'carrots'.

Below: Wing tunnel model with wing bodies.

was to be carried. It was powered by two Armstrong Siddeley Sapphire engines.

Also studied in May 1950 was P317, a scheme for a fighter-bomber version of the basic Javelin. Studies indicated that the aircraft could be developed to carry four 1,000lb bombs externally in two streamlined containers beneath the fuselage.

Other 1950 schemes included P318, a two-seat, long-range rocket-armed fighter; P319, a dual control version; P322, an interceptor development powered by ASSa50 engines; P323, a long-range fighter development of P.322; and P.324, a fighter-bomber and rocket-armed development of P322. The investigation of P319, the dual control version, was initiated by OR278 for a pilot conversion, instrument and gunnery training aircraft. Design studies for both tandem and side-by-side seating were investigated, but in the dual interests of minimum changes to the basic Javelin airframe, and providing the student pilot with a cockpit layout and instrument presentation identical to that which he would find in the operational aircraft, the tandem seat layout was finally selected. The work on P319 led eventually to the Javelin T Mk 3 trainer, for which specification T118D was issued.

A major proposed development of the basic Javelin was for a day and night photographic reconnaissance aircraft to meet OR309. Prepared in January 1952, this was offered in two versions, interim and long term.

The interim version (Scheme 1), P346, used the existing Javelin wing, but had a new fuselage nose extended by 2ft to provide space for the camera equipment.

Internal fuel capacity was increased from 750 to 1,160gal. This, however, even together with 500gal carried externally, was only just sufficient to meet the low level range requirement and fell far short of the high level range. The shape of the rear fuselage was modified to accommodate the special equipment code-named 'Orange Putter' and 'Green Satin', but the aircraft was not able to carry the full range of photographic equipment specified for day operations, owing to cg considerations.

The long term version (Scheme 2), P347, embodied the new fuselage nose of P346, and in addition had new extension wings, increasing the span from 52ft to 66ft. An additional 400 gal of fuel was carried in the extension wings and this, together with an extra tankage in the front fuselage of 240gal, raised the total internal fuel capacity to 1,800gal. Bigger ventral tanks were provided, giving a total overload fuel capacity of 2,550gal, compared with the 1,660gal of the interim version. The tankage enabled the version to meet the

range of requirements, the high level range being achieved with the use of the external tanks, although the requirement was for the specified range on internal fuel. The fuel arrangement on this version enabled the aircraft to be trimmed so that it could carry the full range of photographic equipment required by OR309.

A further design study, P348, was submitted for the long term version. This embodied two 70mm cameras housed in wing leading edge fairings, a position suitable for stereo forward oblique photography, and as an alternative to the single forward facing 70mm camera in the extreme nose of the fuselage.

The additional fuel capacity provided on the later version of the photographic reconnaissance version of the Javelin, was also embodied in a proposal to meet the requirements of specification F5/49 for a high altitude escort fighter with a range of more than 3,300 miles. Other proposals included single and two-seat fighters, armed with bombs and rockets in addition to the normal fixed gun armament.

By far the most significant of the Javelin developments was that for a 'thin-wing' version. TWD experience during the Korean War had shown how difficult it was to make successful interceptions at high speed and altitudes beyond the range of ground control. One solution to the problem would be to use a specialised long-range aircraft which would destroy

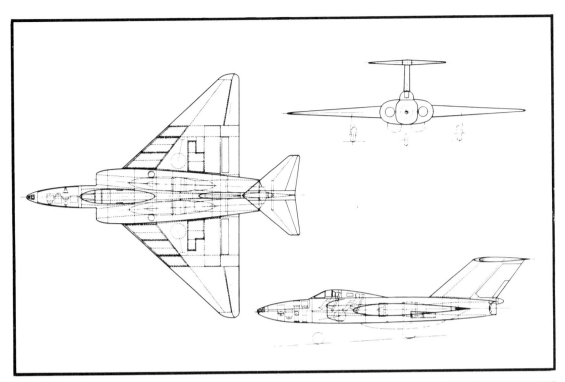

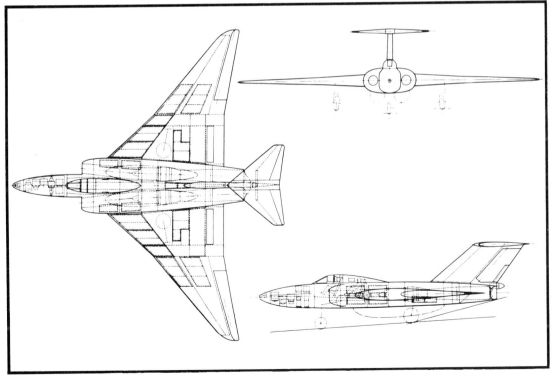

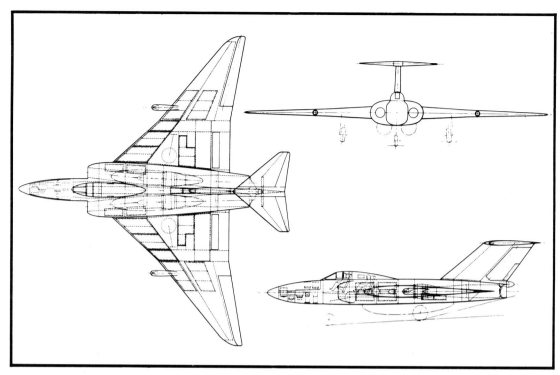

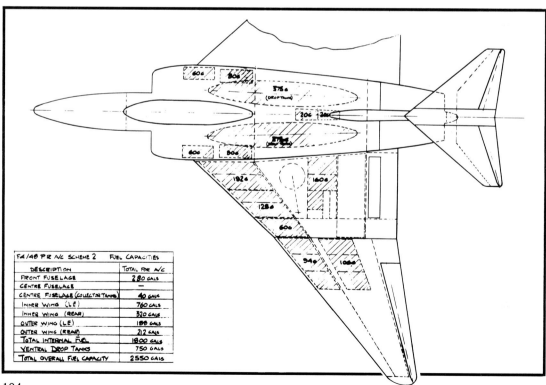

FA/4B P R A/C SCHEME 2	FUEL CAPACITIES
DESCRIPTION	TOTAL FOR A/C
FRONT FUSELAGE	280 GALS
CENTRE FUSELAGE	—
CENTRE FUSELAGE (COLLECTOR TANKS)	40 GALS
INNER WING (LE)	760 GALS
INNER WING (REAR)	320 GALS
OUTER WING (LE)	188 GALS
OUTER WING (REAR)	212 GALS
TOTAL INTERNAL FUEL	1800 GALS
VENTRAL DROP TANKS	750 GALS
TOTAL OVERALL FUEL CAPACITY	2550 GALS

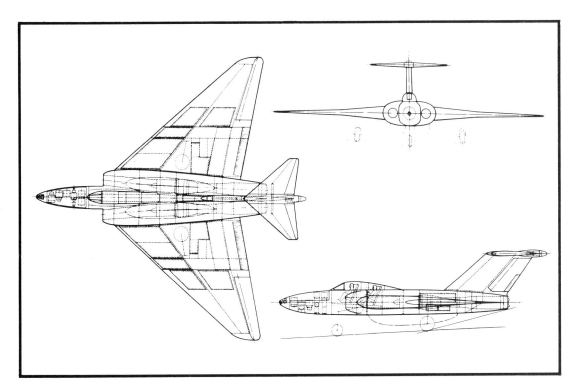

Above left: Gloster Project P348, for a photographic reconnaissance version of the Javelin, embodied two 70mm cameras in wing leading edge fairings.

Left: Location of fuel tanks in Projects P347 and P348.

Above: Gloster Project P350 for a photographic reconnaissance version of the Javelin to meet Specificatioin PR118D and P.

enemy interceptors over their known bases, and bombers early in their outward flight.

The requirements for such a 'bomber support' aircraft were issued in December 1952 as a new air staff Operational Requirement OR234. The specification called for a crew of two, and search radar. Armament was to be cannon, batteries of rockets and guided weapons. A long range was an obvious requirement, as were a high rate of climb, a short take-off and landing lengths.

The requirements posed a formidable challenge, but such was the potential of the basic Javelin, that Glosters were confident that they could be met economically by the development of a bigger, thinner wing, a modified tail unit and the installation of 11,000lb thrust Armstrong Siddeley Sapphire Sa7 engines.

Work started on a project, known as the Javelin 'TWD', to meet OR234.

Early in 1953 specification PR118D and P was issued for a photo-reconnaissance version of the fighter, and Gloster studied ways of accommodating the PR requirements without jeopardising the primary fighter role. These studies culminated in proposal P350 being tendered to the Ministry of Supply on 20 July 1953.

Following extensive wind tunnel testing the TWD now had a wing of 7.5% thickness/chord and was powered by two 12,500lb thrust Sapphire Sa9 engines. The PR version was fitted with up to eight cameras, an array of photoflash equipment, and rearward-looking radar mounted in the fin-tailplane fairing. The day interceptor P356 was armed with two Red Dean and two Firestreak air-to-air missiles, plus two 30mm cannon.

Maximum speed of the PR and day interceptor versions was estimated to be 564kts at 45,000ft, and both had an absolute ceiling of just over 59,000ft and an endurance of 1hr 15min. The night fighter carried similar armament, but had slightly inferior performance; the estimated maximum speed being 561kts at 40,000ft, and the absolute ceiling 58,400ft.

While these proposals were being prepared Bristol had announced a new version of the Olympus engine developing 16,000lb thrust. Gloster lost little time in

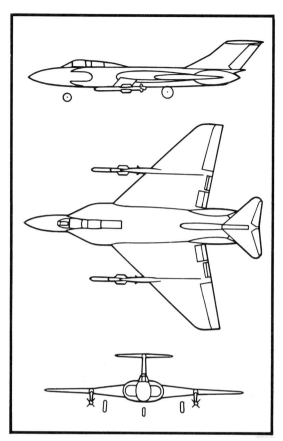

Left: Gloster Project P376, supersonic development of the Javelin concept P153D. Powered by two 20,000lb thrust Bristol 01.21R turbojets with reheat, this had a calculated maximum speed of Mach 1.82 at 36,000ft and a sea level rate of climb of 57,000ft/min.

been put in hand'. The new aircraft would carry 'a still more advanced electronic and guided-weapons system'. The contract for the 18 aircraft was placed on 5 April 1955.

However, the final F153D specification was not received until the following month — more than three years after the original OR was issued. Despite this, design work was proceeding smoothly to a programme established late in 1954, and a large quantity of drawings were released to the workshops. According to this programme the date of the first flight of the prototype was targeted for March 1957.

At this stage, the Gloster project, P370, was a subsonic/transonic aircraft with a long range acquisition radar and an advanced pursuit on collision course weapon system, with 30mm Aden guns as secondary armament.

The tight timescales caused concern in some departments. The engine supplier gave a date of late 1957 for the prototype, with the engines for the pre-production aircraft following a year later. The installation of the Red Dean missile was also a greater problem than initially envisaged and would obviously take longer to develop than estimated.

There was, also, even greater apprehension than normal that the aircraft might not be the right one for the job when it entered service several years hence. The age of the supersonic fighter was being heralded in many quarters.

Thus, in May 1956, with the prospect of further increases in hostile target speeds, Glosters submitted Proposal P376, a supersonic development of the P370, capable of cruising at Mach 1.3. This increase in performance was to be achieved by extending the fuselage fore and aft to improve the area-rule distribution, plus the use of thin wings and tail surfaces of 5% mean thickness/chord ratio. The thin wing idea, however, was abandoned because of the consequent reduction in internal volume available for fuel. The P376 was powered by two Olympus B.01.21R engines which, were expected to develop a total of 29,000lb thrust. The fighter was 72ft long and had a wing span of nearly 61ft. Wing area was 1,235sq ft, and the operational weight over 50,000lb. Wind tunnel tests indicated that the aircraft would have a maximum speed, with reheat, of Mach 1.79 at 45,000ft. At sea level the rate of climb was an astonishing 57,000ft/min. The extensive design effort involved in this project was undertaken by Armstrong Whitworth.

producing a proposal embodying these engines, which was submitted in October 1953.

Further refinements were made during the next four months, and in February 1954 the Sapphire Sa7 had been selected for the prototype TWD and the Olympus B.01.6 for the pre-production aircraft. Barely two months later the Olympus was specified for all aircraft.

During the last half of 1954, the proposals were updated with the latest details of the Olympus B.01.6, B.01.7 and B.01.SR engines. As so often happens during such project developments, the extra engine thrust available does not always improve the performance, but merely maintains it against ever increasing weight. At this stage the estimated combat weight of the TWD had increased to 43,000lb.

In January 1953 the TWD programme was given a major boost when Treasury approval was given for the manufacture of 18 pre-production aircraft. Public news of this was given on 10 March by the Under-Secretary of State for Air who stated 'a later generation all-weather fighter will be developed from the Javelin and a development batch of 18 has already

Various interception 'scenarios' were investigated; one of these envisaged the destruction of an enemy bomber at 50,000ft, 200 nautical miles from base only 23min after take-off.

Drawings were released to the workshop and component manufacturer and sub-assembly operations began. At this stage the first flight of the prototype supersonic F153D was set for December 1958. A detailed mock-up of the complete aircraft was constructed, together with other, smaller units, one of which was a space mock-up of the cockpit which was used by members of the RAF Institute of Aviation Medicine to check the pilots's seat position.

Work continued despite rumours and 'leaks' of a major change in defence policy by the government relating to manned fighter aircraft. These backroom rumours turned into front office fact when, in July 1956 the government officially cancelled the F153D.

This fundamental change in policy was elaborated by Duncan Sandys, Minister of Defence, in the famous White Paper of 1957. This confirmed the government's belief that the day of the manned fighter was coming to an end and that Britian would cease the development of this class of warplane after the Lightning.

The cancellation of the supersonic F153D not only ended the Javelin story; it also heralded the end of the Gloster Aircraft Company itself.

After the cancellation Gloster had no new production contracts in the offing and no new aircraft under development. The company embarked on an ambitious programme to apply the experience gained during 43 years production of military aircraft to the development of civil aircraft.

During the next four desperate years almost all civil avenues were explored, from turbine to piston-engined transports; from executive aircraft to transonic air-

Left: One-fifthteenth scale free flight model of the Gloster P376. The area ruling of the fuselage is evident.

107

liners; V/STOL transports; even an unmanned crop-spraying helicopter. None of these projects bore fruit.

A number of proposals for military aircraft were also schemed, including P504, a proposed conversion of a Meteor T7 for VTOL research, and P505, in 1960, for a strike reconnaissance STOL aircraft to a SHAPE requirement. Of general Javelin configuration this 30,000lb aircraft had one Rolls-Royce Conway RCo11 main propulsion unit and four RB162 lift engines. A feature of special interest of this proposal was the unusual curved leading edge of the 'Lightning-type' sharply swept wing.

In October 1961, Gloster Aircraft Company merged with Sir W. G. Armstrong Whitworth Aircraft Ltd, to form Whitworth Gloster Aircraft Ltd. In July 1963, following a major reorganisation of the Hawker Siddeley Group, the name Gloster disappeared when the company merged with the Avro Whitworth Division of Hawker Siddeley Aviation.

On 6 April 1964, the Hucclecote factory was sold and, with the signature of a pen, the story of Gloster, and the Javelin, came to an end.

Below: The one-fifthteenth scale model with a modified rear end.

Bottom: One-tenth scale low speed wind tunnel model of Gloster Project P376.

Gloster Projects and Proposals Associated with the Javelin Programme:

Jan 1947 Spec F43/46 issued for single-seat day fighter.

Spec F44/46 issued for two-seat night fighter.

P228 1946 Design study for 'Meteor-like' two-seat night fighter to F44/46.

P234 1947 Scheme for delta-wing single-seat day fighter to F43/46.

P238 1947 Scheme for single-seat day and night interceptor.

P240 1947 Scheme for 'plank-winged' day and night interceptor.

P248 1947 Scheme for single-seat interceptor to F43/46.

P250 1947 Scheme for interceptor to F43/46.

Feb 1948 Spec F3/48 for single-seat day fighter.

Spec F4/48 for two-seat night fighter.

P272 1948 Design Study for two-seat night fighter.

P275 1948 Design Proposal for single-seat day fighter to F3/48.

P276 1948 Design Tender for two-seat night fighter to F4/48.

P279 1948 Design Study for two-seat night fighter to F4/48.

P280 1949 Design Study for two-seat day/night fighter to F4/48.

P315 1950 Design Study for two-seat long range fighter.

P316 1950 Design Study for single-seat long range fighter.

P317 1950 Scheme for fighter-bomber Javelin with 4 × 1,000lb bombs.

P318 1950 Scheme for two-seat long range rocket armed fighter.

P319 1950 Scheme for dual control Javelin.

P322 1950 Design Study for Javelin with ASSa50 engines.

P323 1950 Design Study for long-range version of P322.

P324 1950 Design Study for fighter-bomber and rocket armed P322.

P325 1951 Scheme for high-altitude escort fighter.

P346 1952 Design Study of PR development of Javelin — Scheme 1.

P347 1952 Design Study of PR development of Javelin — Scheme 2.

P348 1952 Design Study of P347 with wing cameras.

Dec 1952 Operational Requirement OR234 issued.

Jan 1953 Specification PR118D and P issued.

P350 1952 Tender for PR development of Javelin to PR 118D and P.

P356 1953 Tender for thin-wing development of Javelin.

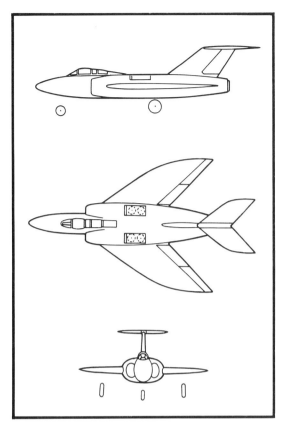

Above: Gloster Project P505, August 1960. Scheme for a tactical strike reconnaissance STOL aircraft to SHAPE requirement GOR2. It was powered by one Rolls-Royce Conway RCo11 main propulsion unit and four RB162 lift engines.

P368 1954 Javelin 1 and 2. Installation of four Blue Jays on underwing pylons.

Specification F153D issued.

P370 1953 Thin-wing development of Javelin with Olympus to F153D. Construction started.

P371 1953 Design Proposal for P370 with two Red Dean missiles.

P372 1953 Design Proposal for P370 with four Firestreak missiles.

P376 1956 Supersonic development of P370 to F153D.

P382 1957 Design Study of Javelin 7 with two Scorpion rocket motors.

P505 1960 Scheme for STOL tactical strike reconnaissance aircraft to GOR 2, based on Javelin concept.

Appendices

1
Javelin Technical Data

Dimensions	Mk 1	Mk 2	Mk 3	Mk 4	Mk 5	Mk 6	Mk 7	Mk 8	Mk 9
Span	52ft 0in (15.8m)	52ft 0in (15.8m)	52ft 0in (15.8m)	52ft 0in (15.8m)	52ft 0in (15.8m)	52ft 0in (15.8m)	52ft 0in (15.8m)	52ft 0in (15.8m)	52ft 0in (15.8m)
Length	56ft 3in (17.1m)	56ft 3in (17.1m)	59ft 11in (18.2m)	56ft 3in (17.1m)	56ft 3in (17.1m)	56ft 3in (17.1m)	56ft 3in (17.1m)	56ft 3in (17.1m)	56ft 9in (17.2m)
Height	16ft 0in (4.8m)	16ft 0in (4.8m)	16ft 0in (4.8m)	16ft 0in (4.8m)	16ft 0in (4.8m)	16ft 0in (4.8m)	16ft 0in (4.8m)	16ft 0in (4.8m)	16ft 0in (4.8m)
Wing area	927sq ft (86sq m)	927sq ft (86sq m)	927sq ft (86sq m)	927sq ft (86sq m)	927sq ft (86sq m)	927sq ft (86sq m)	927sq ft (86sq m)	927sq ft (86sq m)	927sq ft (86sq m)
Weights:									
Take-off (clean aircraft)	31,580lb (14,324kg)	32,100lb (14,500kg)	38,000lb (17,237kg)	32,800lb (14,877kg)	34,990lb (15,871kg)	35,810lb (16,243kg)	35,690lb (16,188kg)	37,410lb (16,968kg)	38,100lb (17,272kg)
Overload (two ventral tanks)	36,690lb (16,641kg)	37,200lb (16,873kg)	42,000lb (19,051kg)	37,480lb (17,000kg)	39,370lb (17,857kg)	40,600lb (18,416kg)	40,270lb (18,266kg)	42,510lb (19,282kg)	43,165lb (19,578kg)
Performance:									
Max speed at sea level (clean aircraft)	616kts (0.925MN) (1,141km/h)	616kts (0.925MN) (1,141km/h)	555kts (0.83MN) (1,028km/h)	610kts (0.915MN) (1,130km/h)	612kts (0.92MN) (1,134km/h)	612kts (0.92MN) (1,134km/h)	616kts (0.925MN) (1,141km/h)	610kts (0.915MN) (1,130km/h)	610kts (0.915MN) (1,130km/h)
Max speed at 35,000ft (10,669m)	—	—	523kts (0.91MN) (969km/h)	—	—	—	—	534kts (0.925MN) (989km/h)	534kts (0.925MN) (989km/h)
Max speed at 40,000ft (12.192m)	540kts (0.94MN) (1,000km/h)	540kts (0.94MN) (1,000km/h)	—	550kts (0.955MN) (1,019km/h)	535kts (0.93MN) (991km/h)	535kts (0.93MN) (991km/h)	—	—	—
Max speed at 45,000ft (13,716m)	—	—	—	—	—	—	540kts (0.945MN) (1,000km/h)	—	—
Climb to 45,000ft (13,716m)	9.8min	9.8min	22min	8min	10.3min	10.3min	6.6min	—	—
Climb to 50,00ft (15,240m)	—	—	—	—	—	—	—	9.25min	9.25min
Service ceiling	52,500ft (16,001m)	52,500ft (16,001m)	46,000ft (14,020m)	50,700ft (15,435m)	50,100ft (15,270m)	50,100ft (15,270m)	52,800ft (16,039m)	52,000ft (15,849m)	52,000ft (15,849m)
Absolute ceiling	55,000ft (16,764m)	55,000ft (16,764m)	49,500ft (15,087m)	52,000ft (15,849m)	51,600ft (15,726m)	51,600ft (15,726m)	54,100ft (16,489m)	54,000ft (16,459m)	54,000ft (16,459m)

Powerplant: Two 8,000lb (3,628kg) thrust Armstrong Siddeley Sapphire Sa6 Mk 10201 (port) and 10301 (starboard) turbojets (Mks 1, 4 and 5).
Two 8,000lb (3,628kg) thrust Armstrong Siddeley Sapphire Sa6 Mk 10701 (port) and 10801 (starboard) turbojets (Mks 2, 5 and 6).
Two 8,000lb (3,628kg) thrust Armstrong Siddeley Sapphire Sa6 Mk 11201 (port) and 11301 (starboard) turbojets (Mk 3).
Two 11,000lb (4,990kg) thrust Armstrong Siddeley Sa7 Mk 20301 (port) and 20401 (starboard) turbojets (Mk 7).
Two 11,000lb (4,990kg) thrust Armstrong Siddeley Sapphire Sa7R Mk 20501R (port) and 20601R (starboard) turbojets with 12% reheat to provide 12,300lb (5,579kg) thrust above 20,000ft (6,096m) altitude (Mk 8).
Two 11,000lb (4,990kg) thrust Armstrong Siddeley Sapphire Sa7R Mk 20901R (port) and 21001R (starboard) turbojets with 12% reheat to provide 12,300lb (5,579kg) thrust above 20,000ft (6,096m) altitude (Mk 9).
Fuel: 765gal (3,475 litres) (Mks 1, 2 and 4); 1,064gal (4,836 litres) (Mk 3); 995gal (4,340 litres) (Mks 5 and 6); 915gal (4,158 litres) (Mk 7); 950gal (4,318litres) (Mks 8 and 9). All variants could carry two 250gal (1,136litres) ventral tanks and Mks 7, 8 and 9 had provision for four 230gal (1,046 litres) tanks on underwing pylons.

Armament: Four fixed Aden 30mm cannon mounted in the outer mainplanes. Mks 7, 8 and 9 also had provision for four de Havilland Firestreak air-to-air guided weapons carried on underwing pylons.
Production: A total of 435 GA5s and Javelins were built; 302 by Gloster Aircraft Co Ltd, Hucclecote, Glos and 133 by Sir W. G. Armstrong Whitworth Aircraft Ltd, Baginton, Coventry.
7 prototypes 1949-54.
40 Javelin Mk 1

30 Javelin Mk 2
22 Javelin Mk 3
50 Javelin Mk 4
64 Javelin Mk 5
33 Javelin Mk 6
142 Javelin Mk 7
47 Javelin Mk 8
116 Javelin Mk 9 (converted from Mk 7 aircraft).

2
Sequence of Javelin Marks into Squadron Service

Mark	Date	Squadron	Mark	Date	Squadron
F(AW) Mk 1	Feb 1956	No 46	F(AW) Mk 7	Dec 1958	No 25
F(AW) Mk 4	Feb 1957	No 141	(4×Firestreak		
F(AW) Mk 5	May 1957	No 151	2×30mm cannon)		
F(AW) Mk 2	June 1957	No 46	T Mk 3	Mar 1959	228 OCU
F(AW) Mk 6	End 1957	No 89	F(AW) Mk 8	Nov 1959	No 41
F(AW) Mk 7	July 1958	No 33	F(AW) Mk 9	Dec 1959	No 25
(4×30mm cannon)			F(AW) Mk 9R	May 1961	No 29

3
Squadron Re-equipment Sequence

Date	Squadron	Re-equipment from/to	Date	Squadron	Re-equipment from/to
Feb 1956	No 46	Meteor NF12/14 to Javelin F(AW) Mk 1	July 1958	No 33	Meteor NF12/14 to Javelin F(AW) Mk 7 (4-gun version)
Feb 1957	No 141	Venom NF3 to Javelin F(AW) Mk 4	Sept 1958	No 64	Meteor NF12/14 to Javelin F(AW)Mk 7 (4-gun version)
April 1957	No 23	Venom NF3 to Javelin F(AW) Mk 4	Dec 1958	No 25	Meteor NF12/14 to Javelin F(AW) Mk 7 (4 Firestreak + 2-gun version)
May 1957	No 151	Venom NF3 to Javelin F(AW) Mk 5)	April 1959	No 72	Meteor NF12/14 to Javelin F(AW) Mk 4 & 5
End 1957	No 89	Venom NF3 to Javelin F(AW) Mk 2 and F(AW) Mk 6 (6 of each mark)	July 1961	No 60	Meteor NF14 to Javelin F(AW) Mk 9
Jan 1958	No 29	Meteor NF11 to Javelin F(AW) Mk 6			

4
Javelin Marks and Squadrons

Mark	Squadron	Mark	Squadron
F(AW) Mk 1	No 46	F(AW) Mk 5	Nos 5, 11, 41, 72, 87, 151
F(AW) Mk 2	Nos 46, 85, 89	F(AW) Mk 6	Nos 29, 46, 85 89
T Mk 3	Nos 3, 5, 11, 23, 25, 29, 33, 41, 46, 60, 64, 72, 85, 87, 151	F(AW) Mk 7	Nos 23, 25, 33, 64
		F(AW) Mk 8	Nos 23, 41, 64, 72, 85
F(AW) Mk 4	Nos 3, 11, 23, 41, 72, 87, 96, 141	F(AW) Mk 9	Nos 5, 11, 23, 25, 29, 33, 60, 64

Acknowledgements

Many people, companies and organisations contribute to a 'documentary' book of this nature. Normally, one of the prime sources of information is the manufacturer of the aircraft. In the case of the Javelin, however, not only is the company concerned, Gloster Aircraft, no longer in existence but, unbelievably, its irreplaceable historical archival data has been almost totally dissipated or destroyed. Those whose task it was to care for this information have failed future generations in a manner which is inexcusable. The people concerned should bear a sense of great guilt.

Thus, in gathering material for this book, I have been more dependent than normal on individuals. I thank all those who supplied information and advice, in particular those whose interest in aviation caused them to acquire and keep information and data more thoroughly than those formally charged with this task.

Among the enthusiasts, special thanks are due to C. Baxter, D. Clarke, M. Kilburn, R. Williams, and my good friend 'Reg' Redford.

Perhaps most important of all, are the contributions from those who flew and supervised the Javelins in the Royal Air Force. The many who provided such information include Flt Lt Cooke, Flt Lt C. Holman, C. Neale, N. F. Penny, M. Stiles and B. Whorwood. Special thanks are due to Grp Capt 'Jock' Fraser AFC, RAF, Retd and Air Cdre M. H. 'Dusty' Miller CBE, AFC, RAF, Retd, for their help in recording the activities of the Javelin during its service in the Far East.

Photographs are an essential part of this book and again having been faced with an almost total lack of 'official' photographs, I am deeply in debt to a large number of individuals.

Among those particular thanks are due to: M. A. Barnes, P. Birtles, D. Clarke, J. Cooke, C. Holman, D. James, W. Heiron, M. Miller, B. Robertson, B. Service, L. Vosloo, B. Whorwood, D. Wilkinson, R. Williams, and my old dear friend John Taylor.

Finally, my thanks to those at the end of the line, without whose assistance, the efforts of the aforementioned would have been in vain; to Joyce and Rose who did the typing and much retyping, and Joy, my wife, for her assistance with proof reading and accepting many lonely hours while the book was being prepared.

Maurice Allward

Left: Refuelling a Javelin in flight was a delicate operation requiring skilful flying in both the fighter and the tanker aircraft. The photograph shows a Javelin F(AW) Mk 9 of No 23 Squadron refuelling from a Valiant tanker of No 214 Squadron.